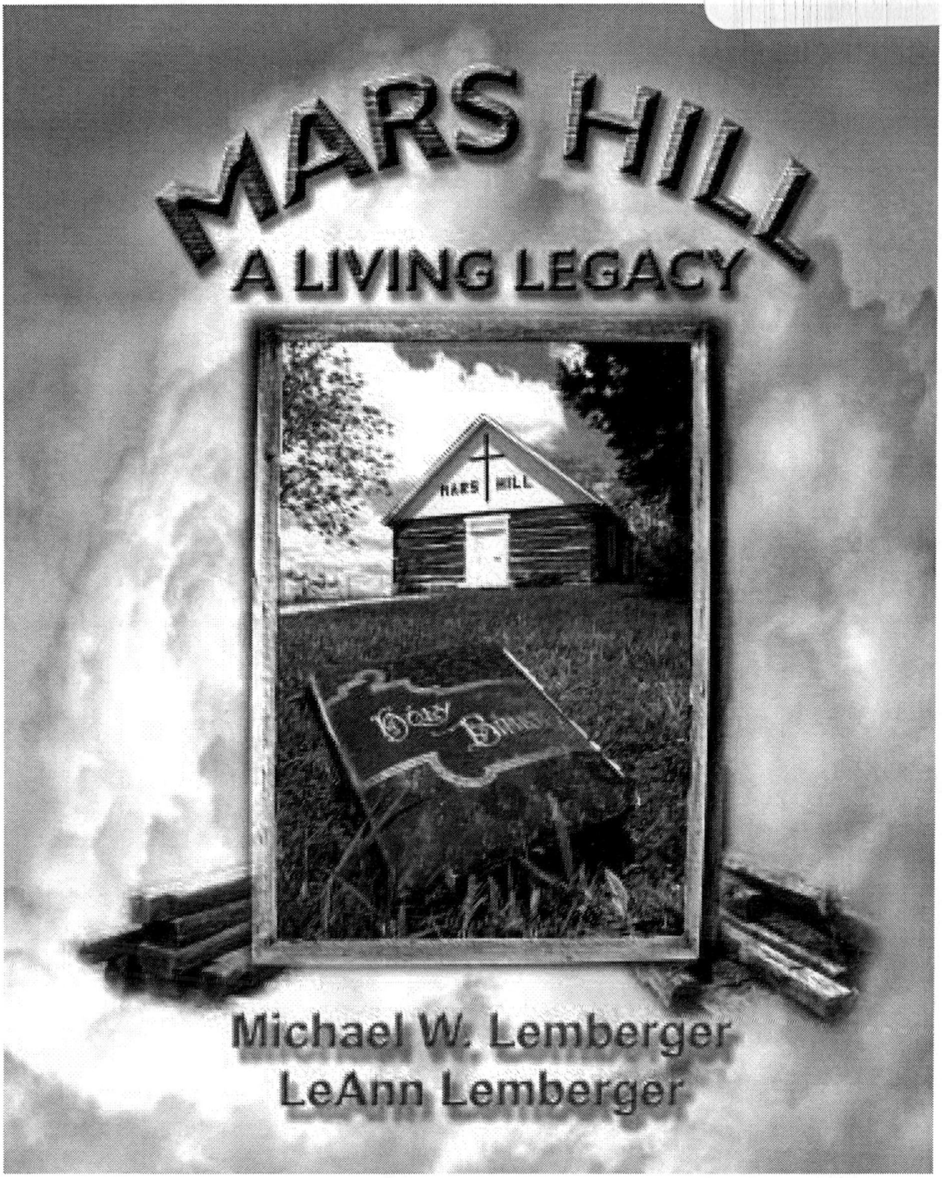
MARS HILL
A LIVING LEGACY
MARS HILL
Michael W. Lemberger
LeAnn Lemberger

PBL Limited
Ottumwa Iowa

# Mars Hill: A Living Legacy

Copyright 2008 by Michael W. Lemberger and LeAnn Lemberger

Cover and design copyright 2008 by Michael W. Lemberger

This edition published 2008
10 9 8 7 6 5 4 3 2 1

ISBN 1-892689-55-3
ISBN 13: 978-1-892689-55-9

Printed in the United States of America

Illustration credits: Front cover -- Mars Hill in 1976, Photo by Michael W. Lemberger. Back cover -- Mars Hill in 2008, Photo by Michael W. Lemberger.

Photographs supplied by Michael W. Lemberger; the Lemberger Collection; Carol Hoffman; Benjamine Post; Geneva Price; Donna Smithhart; Jody Bresch; Larry McCarty; Glen O'Dell; Marge O'Dell.

Poetry credits: "The Old Log Church" (pages 40-41) was previously published in the Mars Hill Church brochures; copyright Pearl Rupe Harness. "The Church on Mars Hill" (page 61) is copyright D.Y. Bevington. "Mars Hill in Iowa" (page 68) was previously published in *The Ottumwa Courier*; copyright Pearl Rupe Harness. "Iowa's Oldest Church -- Mars Hill" (page 79) is copyright Edna M. Shaw. "The Church on Mars Hill Ridge" (page 171) is copyright 2008 by Jody Bresch, used with permission.

All rights reserved. Except for brief passages quoted in any review, the reproduction or utilization of this work in whole or in part, in any form or by any electronic, mechanical, or other means, now known or hereinafter invented, including xerography, photocopying and recording, or in any information storage and retrieval system, is forbidden without the express permission of the publisher. For permission contact:

                    Rights Editor
                    PBL Limited
                    P.O. Box 935
                    Ottumwa IA 52501-0935
                    pbl@pbllimited.com

Copies of this book are available from PBL Limited. See page 174 for details on ordering by mail, or visit our website at www.pbllimited.com for more information.

# Acknowledgements

We wish to thank:

**The Mars Hill Board of Trustees**: Donald Bramschreiber (chairman), Joy Bramschreiber (secretary), Jody Bresch, Larry Crow, Esther Crow, Craig Dooley, Brian Hoffman, Carol Hoffman, Willis Hoffman, Glen O'Dell, Jodi O'Dell, Benjamine Post (treasurer), Geneva Price, Donna Smithhart, Lester Smithhart, and Todd Smithhart.

**The Book Committee:** Carol Hoffman, Brian Hoffman, Benjamine Post, Donna Smithhart, and Geneva Price. Committee members were tireless in seeking out and sharing information, documents, and photographs.

We particularly wish to thank Don Bramschreiber and Donna Smithhart for their immediate enthusiasm when this project was first proposed; Jody Bresch for sharing her manuscript history of Mars Hill; Iowa State Senator Dennis Black for sharing his research about Medal of Honor recipient John Donaldson; Pat Essick of the Ottumwa Public Library for helping locate research materials and memoirs; and local historian Sue Parrish for her enthusiastic support.

The early settlers who built Mars Hill Church had more important things to do than keep records, and after so many years have elapsed, it is sometimes difficult to tell truth from legend. Stories have been told and retold, written and rewritten, and sometimes errors have crept into the transcription or into the memory itself. Names are spelled in various ways, and identities have become confused. In many manuscript histories, facts are reported but no authority is listed, making it difficult to discover the original source. Finding the same information in several different reports does not guarantee that the information is reliable, and some errors have been repeated so frequently that they have become accepted as fact. For instance, we found firm statements that the church was built "before 1846", "about 1850", "in 1856", and "in 1857". We found contradictory stories about the first burials -- who the people were, how they were related, and when and how they died.

We have used the earliest known sources, and wherever we could, we have checked the facts. However, in many cases, it is no longer possible to be certain of what really happened through the 150 years of history witnessed by the log church standing on Mars Hill Ridge.

*--LeAnn & Michael Lemberger*

# Mars Hill Church

In 1957, the 100th anniversary of its construction, the church was featured on the front of the Des Moines Sunday Register's Picture Magazine. The cover art was produced by Frank Miller, the Register's Pulitzer-Prize-winning cartoonist.

## Mars Hill Church

Oldest log church still in occupancy in the United States.

One of the largest log buildings ever erected in Iowa.

A Living Legacy

# Contents

The Beginning   6
Building the Church   12
Early Settlers   16
Before the Civil War   18
The Civil War Years   20
After the War   32
The Turn of the Century   34
Reunions   48
Mid-20th Century   55
Mars Hill Cemetery   91
List of Burials at Mars Hill Cemetery   92
Vandalism & the Occult   118
The Fire   123
Rebuilding   135
The Renewed Church   165
Moving To the Future   168

Mars Hill Church

# THE BEGINNING

The origins of Mars Hill Church – both the congregation and the building – are uncertain, lost in the mists of history. The early pioneers who settled along the dividing line between Wapello and Davis Counties in southeastern Iowa had more important concerns than keeping records. Making a living and raising a family took hard work and long hours.

The first documentary evidence of the existence of a congregation are found in the records of the Iowa Baptist State Convention.

In a summary of the convention records which was published in 1886, the Rev. S. H. Mitchell notes that Mars Hill is listed among several Baptist churches which joined the group, known as The Fox River Association, in 1855. Mitchell states that Mars Hill was organized in 1852, and says there were 32 members in 1855 when this formal record-keeping began.

Though stories handed down in local families give different dates for the construction of the church (some as early as 1846), it seems more likely that church services were very informal at first, with meetings held at the settlers' homes. It's equally likely that the congregation was formally organized several years before the building was actually erected.

By the early 1850s, just a handful of families had settled a few miles northwest of the current site of Floris, near the line dividing Davis and Wapello Counties. One early pioneer, George Monroe, the son of one of the builders of Mars Hill Church, recalled that there were three Clark families, two Smock families, and one family each named Monroe, Tull, and Seaborn, who settled in the area about 1850.

At that time, according to the Wapello County Historical Society, Ottumwa's first courthouse had recently been built, constructed of logs. Chief Wapello, the namesake of Wapello County, and his friend General Joseph M. Street, the Indian agent based in Agency City, had both recently been buried in the garden of the Indian Agency, near the present-day town of Agency. Upstream on the Des Moines River, J.P. Eddy was operating a trading post and ferry which later became the town of Eddyville. Settlers used the river extensively for rafting and flatboating their goods to markets downstream. There were no railroads, and stagecoaches operated regularly along the

# A Living Legacy

**Church and cemetery in 1976**  Photo by Michael W. Lemberger

Deed and receipt for the land where Mars Hill Church stands.
The complete text is opposite.

Territorial Road which ran through Agency, Dahlonega, Kirkville, and Oskaloosa – formerly the Dragoon Trail.

    In about 1856, George Monroe recalled, the settlers began talking seriously of building a church. The congregation's name, and later that of the church, is thought to refer to Acts 17:22: "Then Paul stood in the midst of Mars Hill [in Athens, Greece], and said, Ye men of Athens, I perceive that in all things ye are too superstitious..."

# A Living Legacy

## Barbra (sic) Clark
## Deed of Baptist Church

For and in consideration of the reguard (sic) and esteem I have for Christianity & benevolent institutions I hereby convey to A. Smock S.A. Monroe & A. Clark the Trustees of the Missionary Baptist Church at Mars Hall (sic) and to their successors in office the following tract of land & described by meets and Bounds as follows to wit. Commencing at the South East corner of the South West quarter of the South East quarter of Section Thirty three (33) in Keokuk No. Seventy One (71) Range Thirteen West. Thence North thirteen Rods thence Due West Eighteen & a half rods Thence due South thirteen rods to the South Line of Said Section. Thence East along Said Section Thence East along said Section (sic) Line Eighteen & a half rods to the place of begining (sic), Containing one & a half (1½) acres More or Less. The said Land Lying & being in the State of Iowa & Wapello County to have & to hold the Same for the use of the Said Baptist Church as Long as they Shall continue to use the Said Lot for a church Lot & burry-Ground. And warrant the title against all persons whomsoever. In Testimony thereof I have hereunto Set my hand and Seal This the 16th day of May A.D. 1857.

**Old views of the church, date not known**

In 1857, Barbra (sic) Clark, the wife of Thomas Clark, Sr., deeded an acre of land to three trustees of the church, to be used as a church and "burry-Ground" (cemetery). By that time, however, there had already been burials in the plot which would become Mars Hill Cemetery, including that of Thomas and Barbra Clark's son John, whose stone gives a death date of October 12, 1846. John Clark was 4 years, 7 months and 6 days old.

## Mars Hill Church

Photo by Michael W. Lemberger

**James Clark was buried at Mars Hill in 1854,
just eight years after the first burial and before the church was constructed.**

## A Living Legacy

**The first grave on the site of Mars Hill (John Clark, 1846) is in the left foreground.**

Thomas and Barbra Clark had arrived in south central Iowa in 1846, just a few months before their son died. A native of Pennsylvania, Thomas was the son of a Revolutionary War veteran, and he was a preacher as well as a farmer. They traveled with their eight children by river boat up the Mississippi to Burlington, and then by covered wagon to the Des Moines River. When they arrived, the river valley was under spring flood waters, so they were attracted to the rock bluff above the surging currents. They paid $63.50 for their land, a plot of 50 acres plus a fraction.

John Clark, the youngest of the Clarks' eight children, died shortly after they arrived. Since there was no cemetery, the Clarks buried their son on their own land. Later it was this plot of land that Mrs. Clark donated to the Baptists, with the provision that the congregation build a church and cemetery on it.

The three trustees named in the deed were Abraham Smock, Sanders A. Monroe, and Andrew Clark. S.A. Monroe's son George later wrote that both his father and his uncle, Abraham Smock, came to Iowa in 1851, settling near the current site of Mars Hill Church.

The deed was filed on May 22, 1857, and the most reliable references indicate that construction of Mars Hill Church began soon thereafter.

After five of their sons enlisted in the Civil War, Thomas and Barbra Clark moved on to Owens Valley, California, and spent the rest of their lives there.

Mars Hill Church

# BUILDING THE CHURCH

Though Mars Hills is the oldest log cabin church in continuous use west of the Mississippi River, it was not the first church established in the area. Some of the founders of Mars Hill were members of other churches, and at least one of these congregations assisted the founders of the new church. Chequest Union Church (sometimes known as the United Baptist Church of Christ at Chequest) assisted by ordaining early ministers for Mars Hill and by advising the new congregation. The Chequest church was located at Dunnville, about 10 miles south of Mars Hill -- far enough away that regular church attendance would have been difficult for people living along the county line.

Minutes of the Chequest Union church note that Abraham and Sarah Smock and Sanders A. Monroe and Catherine Monroe became members there in 1852 -- within a year of when they are thought to have moved to the area. In 1853, these members -- along with Thomas Clark, Mrs. Clark, and others prominent in the early history of Mars Hill -- left the Chequest Union Church by letters of dismissal.

This is most likely the time when the Mars Hill congregation was actually formed. In March of 1853, the clerk of the Chequest church notes that a "Request of Brethren Thomas Clark and Sanders A. Monroe, asking help to constitute a church on Soap Creek was granted," and several members of the Chequest church were dispatched to "go to there (sic) aid."

The break was certainly an amicable and less-than-complete one, for even after the formation of the Mars Hill congregation, some members who had formally left the Chequest church were still involved in its affairs. In the minutes of April 1853, a call was made for "peace of the church, wherapon (sic) a difficulty between Brother Thomas Clark and Brother William Baker was presented... and Brother Baker acknowledged himself in fault and made satisfaction."

By late 1853, the Chequest church was sending help to Mars Hill to ordain a preacher -- Brother A. M. Green. In the spring of 1857, the church again sent

*A Living Legacy*

Photo by Michael W. Lemberger

**This view, taken from 15th Street in 2007, shows the rolling hills of the area with Mars Hill Church, barely visible, perched atop the ridge. The pine tree which towers over the surrounding trees at the center of the photo is in the cemetery. The slope in the foreground is thought to be where the skiers pictured on pages 42-45 made their ski run.**

representatives, this time to assist in the ordination of Brother A. Smock. By that time, Mars Hill Church was most likely under construction.

The site of the church is atop the crest of one of the highest hills in southeastern Iowa, with a view in all directions – a typical location for country cemeteries of the period. Early settlers planted trees around the church, including oaks, cedars, pines, and arborvitae. One huge pine towers above the surrounding trees on the ridge like a sentinel, and it can be seen for a distance of several miles.

The road which ran in front of Mars Hill Church at the time was one of the main thoroughfares through south-central Iowa when the building was erected.

With little commercially-cut lumber available, and the cost for transporting materials high, the congregation opted to use the surrounding forest as raw material. Logs for the church were furnished by S.A. Monroe and Abraham Smock. Settlers chopped the trees from the surrounding timber, hewed the logs to shape, hauled some to the mill to be sawed into lumber, and split the shingles. George Monroe recalled that his father, S.A. Monroe, "took up" one corner of the building and Andrew Clark

## Mars Hill Church

another corner. Constructing the corners of the log structure was crucial to the stability of the building, helping to account for its solidity through the following century and more. Wooden pins held the oak and walnut logs together; there were no nails in the entire structure. The cracks between the logs were filled with clay and plaster chinking.

The completed church measured 28 feet by 26 feet by 10 feet high, making it one of the largest log buildings ever built in Iowa. The logs were as much as 16 inches square, and many of the logs were long enough to run the full length or width of the structure, with no seams. Two 12-pane windows were placed on each side wall. There was only one door; an old tale says that Barbra Clark, the donor of the land, said that there should be only one door because "there is only one way to Heaven."

The church was apparently first heated by a fireplace built of stone hauled from the Des Moines River, with a chimney made of mud and sticks. The fireplace was later replaced with a stove.

---

It was in 1857 that a plot of land was set aside for a cemetery and church to become known as Mars Hill.

One can only think of the preparation that went on during the winter before the building actually took place. The many man hours of physical labor by men and boys working tirelessly to fell the oak trees, trim them and hew them into square logs and with teams of horses dragging them up to the top of the hill where the structure would be erected can only be guessed. Their dedication can only be speculated.

What an exciting time for everyone in the community as they gather on the day when the men would start measuring and notching the logs to fit together. The men and boys worked at different tasks, the women were most likely setting up the plank tables arid either setting out or cooking the food over the open fire for lunch. The young girls were most likely given the task of watching the little ones. You can almost hear the loud "Amens" and joyous chorus as the first logs were notched and placed together. Then slowly as each log was notched and placed, they were able to watch the church take form. How long it took, we today can only guess of the physical labors and hours of work. But the joy that must have sprung from the hearts of the people when they were able to sit inside and sing praises to the Lord, we can be sure was gracious and full of blessings.

– Benjamine Post, Letter to the Editor

## A Living Legacy

Meetings were held on the third weekend of each month, with a service on Saturday night and two services on Sunday (day and evening). The first preachers were A. M. Green, Abraham Smock, John Ferguson, Francy McCune, Joseph Cheetam, and others.

Early male members of the church (most often referred to by other members as "Uncle") were Sanders Monroe, Asa Monroe, Andrew Kae, Thomas Clark, and John William Monroe. Early women members (called "Aunt") included Barbra Clark, Catherine Monroe, Sarah Smock, Hanna Smock, Debby Seaburn and Margaret Anderson Page. Unlike most other churches of the period, men and women were encouraged to sit together.

Rev. Mitchell says in his history of the early Baptist conventions that in 1856, A. Smock was preaching. In 1857, he lists the preacher as J. Farquarson and says 27 baptisms were reported – an enormous increase for a church which just two years before had a reported total membership of 32. In 1859, the pastor listed at Mars Hill was Rev. Ezekiel Kinman, who was also listed as pastor of the church in Bloomfield.

Lemberger Collection

**Mars Hill, front entrance -- thought to be before 1930**

Aaron Post (right)

Anson Brooks &
Mary Patience Thomas Brooks

Isaac Laughridge

# EARLY SETTLERS

In an early memoir of the church, George Monroe, the son of one of the builders of Mars Hill, remembered the names of the earliest area settlers as Smock, Monroe, Tull, Clark, and Seaborn, but in the years after the church was built, other names came to prominence in the neighborhood as well.

Among the early settlers of the region and members of Mars Hill Church were

# A Living Legacy

William Monroe and his wife Phebe Parham Monroe. William was born in 1788 in Rutherford County, North Carolina, and served in the War of 1812. William died in 1863 and is buried at Mars Hill cemetery. In 1878, Phebe applied for a widow's pension based on his military service, but her application was rejected due to a lack of living witnesses.

Her application states that William Monroe enlisted at New Castle, Kentucky in August 1813, to serve

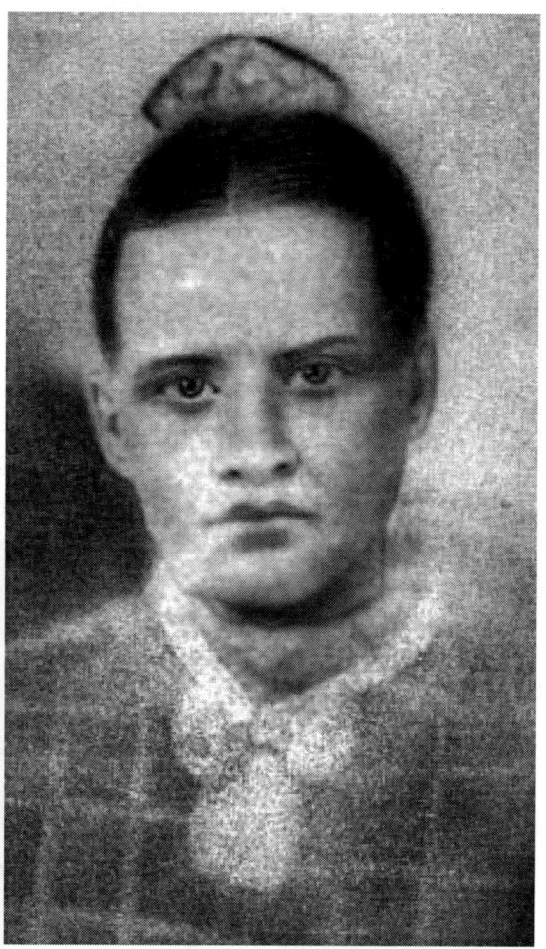

Sarah Garrison,
wife of George Laughridge

for a three-month term; he actually served four weeks and was honorably discharged after cutting his leg near Cincinnati. At the time of his enlistment he was 23 years old, five feet ten inches tall and weighing 160 pounds, with dark brown hair, gray eyes and a fair complexion.

**Aaron Post (left)**

# BEFORE THE CIVIL WAR

Reports vary as to the size of the congregation through the early years. Some sources say the church never was larger than 100 members, though others state that the Sunday School once had as many as 120 members.

It is said that John Brown of abolitionist fame spoke in the church, and local tradition says that Mars Hill was used as a station on the Underground Railroad. Stories which have been handed down through families tell of slaves being smuggled in from the South, hiding out in the timber around the church during the day and then returning to the building at nightfall to be transported farther north under cover of darkness. Several early settlers recalled being told specifics, including that refugees were moved from a house near Drakesville to the church, then on to Eldon which was the next station stop.

However, direct written documentation is hard to find, and some of what exists is clearly in error. One often-quoted source says, "John Brown of Harper's Ferry fame is supposed to have hidden two wagonloads of slaves there [in the church] during the Civil War", but Brown was hanged in 1859, well before the Civil War started. This story may be simply wishful thinking, or the incident might actually have happened, but at an earlier time than has been reported.

The most reliable evidence seems to come from a book published by the Federated Women's Clubs of Davis County in the 1920s. The book quoted George Monroe, whose father settled in the area in 1851 and helped build the church, as saying that John Brown spoke in the church and that it was a station on the Underground Railroad. The Bloomfield *Democrat* reported in 1925 that a former slave who had passed through Mars Hill Church while escaping to freedom had attended a reunion at the church, but did not quote him directly.

An application has been made to the National Parks Service to have Mars Hill Church listed on the National Parks Service's Trail of Stations on the Underground Railroad, but oral tradition is not enough to establish the claim. Further written documentation from the period, such as Bible entries, personal diaries, or letters that describe specific incidences of Underground Railroad activity, remains elusive.

## A Living Legacy

### Chelsea Beamon and Ian Bresch

Chelsea Beamon was a piano student of mine. She had natural grace, meticulous good manners, and a shy benevolent charm. I shared with her mother, Juanita, that I had written a story ["Jocoa's Quilt", about a black child rescued from slavery via the Underground Railroad] and hoped she would allow Chelsea to pose for photos as the main character.

Chelsea, my young son Ian, Juanita and I plotted to get out of bed before the sun rose on a blustery autumn morning and make a trip to Mars Hill Church for a photo op. It was about 4:00 A.M. when we met at Chelsea's house. When we arrived at the church, there was nothing spooky about it, but with the wind tearing across the ridge it was bitter cold. Both of the children had long underwear on under their clothes, but they still had to be miserably uncomfortable. There were no complaints though.

We laughed and giggled about how nuts we were to be out there taking pictures when we could be snuggled up at home warm in our beds. We took photos inside and outside the church, in front and in back, and in the graveyard amongst the tombstones. I had thought to bring a lantern with a candle in it for some light, but we had a wicked time keeping it lit, the wind was so fierce. Chelsea was a delightful model to work with ... There was something pensive in her expression, as if she was really thinking about what it must have been like to be taken from your bed in the middle of the night and set on the trail towards something intangible called "freedom."

*----Jody Bresch*

## THE CIVIL WAR YEARS

Regular services were held in the church until 1861, when the Civil War interrupted normal life. In 1862, with church membership at about 80, Mars Hill saw a number of its young men march off to war, many of them joining the 7th Iowa Cavalry.

George Monroe recalled, "When the Civil War broke out and the call came for volunteers, there were 35 men who attended church here that went to the army. The first one that died and was brought back was Daniel Monroe, one of my brothers. He enlisted in the 15th Iowa Infantry and got as far as Keokuk, took the measles and they settled on his brain and they sent him home to die. He lived a few days after he got home and then died and was buried in this cemetery. This was in February 1862."

**Wesley Soul Monroe, one of the Mars Hill men who served in the Union forces during the Civil War. The backwards "C" on his cap (in left hand) indicates that the image may have been flipped when the original photograph was produced.**

---

Clark, Kees. Age 27. Residence Floris, nativity Pennsylvania. Enlisted Oct. 15, 1861. Mustered Nov. 1, 1861. Promoted Fifth Corporal April 9, 1863; First Corporal June 7, 1863. Mustered out July 24, 1865, Louisville, Ky.

Duffield, Edmund. (Veteran.) Age 22. Residence Bloomfield, nativity Ohio. Enlisted Aug. 17, 1861, as Company Quartermaster Sergeant. Mustered Sept. 4, 1861. Promoted Second Lieutenant Sept. 5, 1862. Promoted First Lieutenant Aug. 23, 1864. Discharged May 15, 1865.

A Living Legacy

Fairburn, William. (Veteran.) Age 22. Residence Floris, nativity Ireland. Enlisted Dec. 1, 1861. Mustered Dec. 1, 1861. Promoted Sixth Corporal July 1, 1862; Fourth Corporal July 11, 1862; Fifth Sergeant June 7, 1863. Re-enlisted and re-mustered Nov. 18, 1863. Promoted Fourth Sergeant May 1, 1864; First Sergeant Nov. 19, 1864; Second Lieutenant Dec. 15, 1864; First Lieutenant Jan. 31, 1865; Captain April 9, 1865. Mustered out July 24, 1865, Louisville, Ky.

Harward, James M. Age 18. Residence Floris, nativity Ohio. Enlisted Aug. 18, 1862. Mustered Sept. 2, 1862. Died of disease Feb. 7, 1863, Helena, Ark.

Monroe, Felix M. Age 17. Residence Floris, nativity Indiana. Enlisted Nov. 25, 1862. Mustered Dec. 18, 1862. Promoted Seventh Corporal Oct. 21, 1864; Sixth Corporal Jan. 9, 1865. Transferred to Company C, Seventh Cavalry Reorganized.

Monroe, John V. Age 34. Residence Floris, nativity Indiana. Enlisted Nov. 5, 1862, as Company Commissary Sergeant. Mustered Dec. 17, 1862. Promoted First Sergeant Oct. 21, 1864. Transferred to Company C, Seventh Cavalry Reorganized.

Monroe, Wesley S. Age 36. Residence Floris, nativity Kentucky. Enlisted Feb. 1, 1863. Mustered Feb. 4, 1863. Promoted Second Sergeant Sept. 9, 1863. Discharged June 25, 1864, Omaha, Neb.

Records of some of the Mars Hill men who served in the Civil War have been reproduced from the Roster and Record of Iowa Soldiers (above).

Photo by Michael W. Lemberger

**Graves of William Smock and Abraham Smock, Mars Hill Cemetery. Abraham Smock, one of the original three trustees, helped to cut the logs for the church and was an early preacher there.**

Monroe goes on, "The next one was Abraham Smock who enlisted in the 7th Iowa Cavalry. He got as far as Davenport, took sick and died and was brought back here for burial. They buried him by the side of the church that he helped to build. This was in May 1863."

In his summary of the Baptist convention records, Rev. Mitchell quotes the 1863 obituary report, which he says "mentions the 'departure to his reward of one who... came to be known by the testimony he had left in all this region, as one of God's noblemen.' This was *Elder Abraham Smock*. He had been for several years 'Moderator of this Association, and was much beloved by all who knew him... He had given two sons to the service of his country, and although at that age of life when one clings with greater tenacity to home and the retirements of private life, he left his quiet retreat and the peaceful duties of the ministry, and entered the service' where 'he died of disease in Camp McClellan, with the words of faith and triumph on his lips, trusting in the Lord Jesus.'" Abraham Smock is buried in the cemetery at Mars Hill.

---

McCaulley, Samuel J. Age 21. Residence Davis County, nativity Ohio. Enlisted April 28, 1862. Mustered April 28, 1862. Died May 25, 1863. Buried in National Cemetery, Springfield, Mo. Section 10, grave 56. See Company D.

# A Living Legacy

Photo by Michael W. Lemberger

Mars Hill Cemetery, from a window of the church (under reconstruction). The grave of John Donaldson, Medal of Honor recipient, is marked by the white stone and flag.

> **Clark, Milton S.** (Veteran.) Age 21. Residence Ottumwa, nativity Pennsylvania. Enlisted June 13, 1861. Mustered Aug. 3, 1861. Wounded May 2, 1863, Chalk Bluff, Mo. Re-enlisted and re-mustered Jan. 1, 1864. Promoted Eighth Corporal Jan. 1, 1864; First Corporal Nov. 25, 1864; Fifth Sergeant Jan. 1, 1865; Third Sergeant Feb. 17, 1865; Second Sergeant June 13, 1865. Mustered out Feb. 15, 1866, Austin, Texas.
>
> **Clark, Thomas.** Age 25. Residence Ottumwa, nativity Pennsylvania. Enlisted June 13, 1861. Mustered Aug. 3, 1861. Discharged for disability March 24, 1862, Butler, Mo.
>
> **Clark, William.** (Veteran.) Age 22. Residence Ottumwa, nativity Pennsylvania. Enlisted June 13, 1861. Mustered Aug. 3, 1861. Re-enlisted and re-mustered Jan. 1, 1864. Mustered out Feb. 15, 1866, Austin, Texas.
>
> **Crandall, Horace S.** Age 44. Residence Wapello County, nativity New York. Enlisted Feb. 12, 1864. Mustered Feb. 26, 1864. **Died at home on sick furlough, Oct. 29, 1864.**

In the records for 1864, Rev. Mitchell does not mention Mars Hill specifically but observes that the records reflect, "The distracted condition of the country absorbs everything."

A Congressional Medal of Honor recipient is buried in the Mars Hill Cemetery, next to the church in the first row of stones. John Donaldson, a native of Pennsylvania, was a sergeant in Company L, 4th Pennsylvania Cavalry. He was awarded the medal after he captured the regimental flag of the 4th Virginia Cavalry during action at Appomattox Court House on April 9, 1865, shortly before the cessation of hostilities. Since the regimental flag was a primary means of communicating with the troops in warfare of the time, capturing it meant the Confederate troops were thrown into disarray and they scattered. Later that day, Confederate General Robert E. Lee surrendered his army to Union general Ulysses S. Grant. Donaldson survived the war and later moved to southern Iowa. He died in 1920.

The list of Mars Hill men who died in the Civil War is a long one. Those buried at Mars Hill cemetery in addition to Daniel Monroe and Abraham Smock include William Smock, Joseph Ryan, and John Anderson.

Not all the Civil War casualties were on Southern battlefields. Anderson was killed in Nebraska while with the 7th Iowa Cavalry. His death was reported in a letter from the company's assistant surgeon, Dr. James W. LaForce – also from the Mars Hill area – to Sanders A. Monroe of Davis County, a brother-in-law of Anderson's.

# A Living Legacy

> **Smock, William J.** Age 21. Residence Floris, nativity Indiana. Enlisted June 13, 1861. Mustered Aug. 3, 1861. Died of disease July 14, 1864, Little Rock, Ark. Buried in National Cemetery, Little Rock, Ark. Section 1, grave 723.

The grave of Medal of Honor recipient John Donaldson, at Mars Hill

Photo by Michael W. Lemberger

> **Smith, Lewis.** Age 24. Residence Floris, nativity Ohio. Enlisted June 13, 1861. Mustered Aug. 3, 1861. Died June 25, 1864, Floris, Iowa.
>
> **Ryan, Joseph.** Age 44. Residence Ottumwa, nativity Ohio. Enlisted Jan. 1, 1862. Mustered Jan. 1, 1862. Killed in battle April 6, 1862, Shiloh, Tenn.
>
> **Reynolds, James H.** Age 25. Residence Davis County, nativity Indiana. Enlisted Feb. 16, 1864. Mustered Feb. 16, 1864. Mustered out July 24, 1865, Louisville, Ky.
>
> **Rupe, John M.** Age 18. Residence Wapello County, nativity Iowa. Enlisted Feb. 17, 1864. Mustered Feb. 17, 1864. Mustered out Aug. 24, 1865, Devall's Bluff, Ark.
>
> **Peden, James.** (Veteran.) Age 30. Residence Floris, nativity Ohio. Enlisted Aug. 17, 1861. Mustered Sept. 4, 1861. Promoted Eighth Corporal Feb. 27, 1863; Seventh Corporal July 31, 1863; Third Corporal Jan. 1, 1864. Re-enlisted and re-mustered Feb. 1, 1864. Mustered out Aug. 9, 1865, Atlanta, Ga.
>
> **Hale, Greenville.** Age 43. Residence Ottumwa, nativity Ohio. Enlisted Jan. 4, 1864. Mustered Jan. 4, 1864. Taken prisoner April 25, 1864, Mark's Mills, Ark. Exchanged Feb. 25, 1865. Mustered out Aug. 24, 1865, Devall's Bluff, Ark.

**Hale, Hiram.** Age 38. Residence Ottumwa, nativity Ohio. Enlisted Jan. 4, 1864. Mustered Jan. 4, 1864. Taken prisoner April 25, 1864, Mark's Mills, Ark. Exchanged Feb. 25, 1865. Mustered out May 27, 1865, Davenport, Iowa.

**Hale, John.** Age 26. Residence Ottumwa, nativity Ohio. Enlisted Jan. 4, 1864. Mustered Jan. 4, 1864. Mustered out May 27, 1865. Davenport, Iowa.

**Meek, John W.** Age 35. Residence Floris, nativity Ohio. Enlisted March 10, 1863, as Company Quartermaster Sergeant. Mustered April 3, 1863. Transferred to Company D, Seventh Cavalry Reorganized.

**Monroe, William N.** Age 22. Residence Ottumwa, nativity Indiana. Appointed First Lieutenant March 5, 1863. Mustered April 28, 1863. Resigned Aug. 23, 1864. See Company I, First Cavalry.

**Dr. Laforce's letter to Sanders Monroe:**

Hospital, Ft. Cottonwood, Nebraska Territory. Sept. 20, 1864

Dear Uncle:—I am under the painful necessity of reporting to you the death of two men, Co. C, 7th Iowa Cavalry, John Anderson and William Mosier, of Ashland. They were killed September the eighth about three o'clock in the afternoon of that day by the Indians.

The facts or circumstances were these: Captain Mitchell, John Anderson, Avon Blair, William Mosier, Crandal, and Buford Starkey, a man of Co. F., 7th Iowa Cavalry, took a wagon and a span of horses and went to the canyon or hills, to gather plums, all being well armed with revolvers and Anderson had his carbine besides.

They went up the canyons seven or eight miles and not finding plums as they had expected, they undertook to cross the ridges and come back down another canyon with which they were acquainted, but after reaching the ridge and winding around several miles, they discovered Indians, 50 or 60 in number, about a mile off coming as fast as their ponies could carry them, yelling their war cry.

The Captain directed that they should drive as fast as their horses could go till they were near some ravine, and let the team go, concealing themselves if possible.

The team was started at full speed, Blair, Crandal and Starkey, being out at the time and on ahead. As the team came up, Blair and Starkey got in the wagon. Crandal made for a ravine and concealed himself. A few yards on Blair was thrown out and ran for a ravine, just reaching it as an arrow passed his body and stuck in the bank. Then he concealed himself.

A few hundred yards further on the Captain was thrown out on an open spot of ground on the point of a hill, near a ravine and just had time to pitch himself in a deep little cut hardly sufficient to cover his body, when the Indians passed over the brow of the hill and went thundering on after the wagon. In a minute or so longer the Indians were up with the wagon, so close that the shooting commenced, and the Captain thinks lasted three or four minutes, 40 to 60 shots fired daring the time. We found the boys yesterday about three or four hundred yeards (sic) from where the Captain was concealed.

Mosier's body was found dead, naked, and scalped, near the truck of the wagon, apparently just where he left the wagon for an open ravine near by. Starkey, in the same condition a hundred yards below or down the hollow. Anderson 80 to 100 yards still lower down near a little bunch (not enough to cover his body) of brush which grew against a bank. I think he was badly wounded before he reached the spot where he died, as he seemed to have fought them there some time. He was scalped and naked except his boots. His back was stuck with seven arrows. The shafts and one point I will send home at some convenient opportunity. The other points I left in his body, as they could not be taken out without cutting deep into the flesh. Anderson also seemed to have been shot 5 or 6, possibly 7 or 8 times, with bullets, one of which broke his left arm near the shoulder, which must have disabled him almost entirely before he received his last shot.

The arrows were shot into him after his clothes were taken off. He was also shot in the back of the head, the muzzle of the piece being placed to his head. The attack was a complete surprise as the scouts had brought in no reports of Indians before the boys went out. Probably a wandering band, who gathered up dead and wounded and passed on, as we saw no signs of them when we went out from the fort after the bodies. Captain Mitchell, Blair and Crandal reached the fort under cover of darkness the night after the fight. The bodies were buried here at this fort, "Killed in action, cause of death."

I leave you to tell your sister, Anderson's wife, these particulars. It is too painful a task for me to write it to her. My best regards to all the family. Your son, Newton, and the others are well. Very sincerely,

Asst. Surgeon, Co. C, 7th Iowa Cav."

## Mars Hill Church

```
COMPANY "C"
LaForce, James W.  Rejected Nov. 13, 1862, by Mustering Officer.
```

Dr. James W. LaForce was born in Woodford County, Kentucky, in 1826. His boyhood was spent in Wapello and Davis Counties. Always adventurous, he went to California and to Colorado before the Civil War, seeking gold. He studied medicine at the University of Iowa, and he practiced in Wapello and Davis Counties, living at Agency, Eldon, and Floris.

During the Civil War period, LaForce was rejected on his first attempt to enlist, but eventually he served more than two years as assistant surgeon with the 7th Iowa Cavalry in western Nebraska before being invalided home on account of his eyes.

Lemberger Collection

## A Living Legacy

Years later, Mrs. LaForce, then living in Eldon, Iowa, wrote her recollections of the Civil War era at Mars Hill, and she read her story for the Decoration Day program given at the church on May 30, 1916. Her account (which includes errors) follows:

### MARS HILL IN WAR TIMES
### by Mrs. J. W. LaForce

"It was in the month of May, 1858, that I first worshiped in the then new sanctuary of Mars Hill. I do not know the date of the organization of the church, nor the names of its members, but how well I remember that day, so long ago. Rev. Ferguson was the preacher. On the front amen seat in the corner, next to the congregation, sat Uncle Tommy Clark, the senior Deacon. Uncle Tommy was the embodiment of the law, and woe betide the backsliding members who failed to attend the church meeting on the third Sunday of the month. Next to him sat Archibald Smock, next Abraham Smock, a preacher of mean ability, but not, at that time, pastor of the church. Next to him and next to the wall sat Uncle Sanders (all of the elderly men were called Uncle) A. Monroe, deacon, who was then and still is the embodiment of the gospel; on the seat back of them sat Andrew Kee and Thomas Clark, Wm. Kandy Tull and John Anderson; on the back seat sat Wm. and Nuton Clark, Wm. Newton Monroe, Wm. Smock and Charlie Smock.

On the opposite side sat Aunt (they were old aunts) Barbara Clark, Catharine Monroe, Sarah Smock, Hannah Smock and Debby Seaburn. On the next seat were Margaret, wife of John Anderson, and the wives of Andrew and Kees Clark, and Tom Kandy Tull. On the back seat sat Lucy Ann Monroe ... the wives of James Reynolds and Chas. Smock.

In the body slips sat a goodly congregation ... The little cemetery outside had not more than a dozen graves in it. The first persons buried there were, I believe, James Clark and his little son who died of cholera in 1854 [sic].

We will pass over to 1861 when the great storm of war struck this

---

Smock, Abraham. Age 44. Residence Floris, nativity Indiana. Enlisted Jan. 1, 1863. Mustered Jan. 1, 1863. Died of disease June 3, 1863, Davenport, Iowa.

Smock, Felix T. Age 17. Residence Floris, nativity Indiana. Enlisted Nov. 25, 1862. Mustered Dec. 18, 1862. Promoted Eighth Corporal July 19, 1864; Sixth Corporal Oct. 13, 1864; Fifth Corporal Jan. 9, 1865. Transferred to Company C, Seventh Cavalry Reorganized.

## Mars Hill Church

> Hastings, Enoch. Age 47. Residence Foris, nativity Pennsylvania. Enlisted Oct. 15, 1861. Mustered Nov. 1, 1861. Transferred to company K Feb. 1, 1862. See company K.

devoted congregation and carried off its members, Wm. N. Monroe, Wm. L. Smock, Charles Smock, and Thomas, Wm. and Wilton Clark. In a few weeks another call took John and Edmond Duffield and James Peden. Still another call and two sons of Aron Smith, Wm. Staken, Hiram Hale, Green Hale and John Hale went but not being personally acquainted with them I am not certain as to the time of their going. The next call Willie Fairburn, Daniel L. Monroe, Madison Harward, Samuel L. McCanley, Joseph Ryan and Kees Clark went. The first soldier buried here was Daniel L. Monroe, he was taken sick with measles at Keokuk and was sent home to die. How well the older ones among us remember the light haired, laughing eyed, lad we laid to rest here that cold day in Feb. 1862. How our hearts went out in sympathy to these devoted parents.

Recruits were called for and Joseph McCouley, Horace Crandle and James Reynolds went. Still another call came and John Anderson, John V. Monroe, Wesley S. Monroe, John Meak, Felix T. Smock, Felix M. Monroe, Ben Kath, Ben Hastings, James W. LaForce and the worthy pastor of the church, Abraham Smock went.

Mr. Smock was a man of fine bodily presence with a great warm hand that beckened [sic] the warm heart behind it. But he was not permitted to face the enemy but was called to his reward very soon. He died at Davenport, May, 1863 and his body was brought back and laid beside the church his hands had helped to build, and for whose spiritual welfare he had beloved and prayed.

Of the brave men who went from this church and congregation, Wm. Smock, Joseph Ryan, Samuel L. McCanley, Madison Farward and John Anderson are buried in the beautiful cemeteries provided for her dead by the nation, and today strangers lay wreaths of flowers on their graves just as we decorate the graves of those who have no kindred near to perform

> Monroe, Daniel. Age 18. Residence Floris, nativity Indiana. Enlisted Dec. 10, 1861. Mustered Dec. 10, 1861. Died of congestion of brain Feb. 6, 1862, Wapello County, Iowa.

> **Smock, Charles.** (Veteran.) Age 18. Residence Floris, nativity Indiana. Enlisted Dec. 18, 1861. Mustered Dec. 18, 1861. Re-enlisted and re-mustered Jan. 1, 1864. Promoted First Sergeant Dec. 19, 1864; Second Lieutenant April 9, 1865; First Lieutenant April 9, 1865. Mustered out July 24, 1865, Louisville, Ky.

that office for them. Of those who returned, Edmond Duffield, Felix Smock, Horace Crandle, Ben Hatch, Louis Smith and John Hale lie buried here. Kees Clark at Chequest, Ben Hastings at Pierce Burying grounds, Wm and Nuton Clark in far off California. It is possible I may have overlooked some with whom I was personally acquainted....

Of the good men and true who went from other states but who have found their last resting place here are Wm. Hamilton, of the 3rd Pennsylvania heavy artillery, and Porter Baird of an Ohio regiment. Let us who came to this festival of the dead not only remember the brave strong men who went out but also cherish the persons and memory of the good fathers, mothers and wives who sent their beloved ones to save their land and nation. Strangers have professed to write the history of Wapello and Davis Counties, but I doubt if the writers knew of the existence of this loyal church whose congregation never numbered even a hundred souls, but which gave to its country 35 men and whose lives went out from sheer exhaustion."

> **McCaulley, Joseph.** (Veteran.) Age 18. Residence Bloomfield, nativity Indiana. Enlisted Aug. 28, 1862. Mustered Aug. 28, 1862. Re-enlisted and re-mustered Feb. 1, 1864. Promoted Eighth Corporal Jan. 1, 1865; Seventh Corporal March 15, 1865; Sixth Corporal May 1, 1865; Fifth Corporal July 1, 1865. Mustered out Aug. 9, 1865, Atlanta, Ga.
>
> **Pilcher, Thomas J.** Age 19. Residence Davis County, nativity Iowa. Enlisted May 11, 1864. Mustered June 4, 1864. Mustered out Sept. 28, 1864, Davenport, Iowa, expiration of term of service.
>
> **Stadter, John W.** Age 17. Residence Davis County, nativity Germany. Enlisted Feb. 15, 1864. Mustered Feb. 26, 1864. Taken prisoner April 25, 1864, Mark's Mills, Ark. Died of disease while a prisoner Aug. 22, 1864, Tyler, Texas. Buried in National Cemetery, Alexandria, La. Section 32, grave 58.
>
> **Anderson, John.** Age 34. Residence Floris, nativity Indiana. Enlisted Dec. 10, 1862. Mustered Dec. 17, 1862. Killed in action Sept. 18, 1864, Fort Cottonwood, Neb. Buried in National Cemetery, Fort McPherson, Colo.

## Mars Hill Church

A Sunday School record from 1885 notes that attendance was 48, and the amount contributed in the collection that week was 69 cents.

## AFTER THE WAR

Though services resumed at Mars Hill after the Civil War, by about 1873 most of the remaining members transferred their membership to the newly-formed Floris Baptist Church. After that, though the Mars Hill congregation became inactive, the church was still used for weddings, funerals, and yearly gatherings.

Lemberger Collection

In 1899, a collection was taken to raise money to replace the church roof.
The record book was left in the church for many years,
where it was nibbled by mice (top left)

# TURN OF THE CENTURY

In 1903, a group of men headed by Frank Agee of Ottumwa put flooring in the old church. The floor remained until the 2006 fire which badly damaged the building.

By 1915, the foundation of the church was in need of repair, so J. E. Crist and his son Ottis E. Crist, Dougless Clark, Dave Clark, and George Gordon put a new foundation under the old structure. Besides the Crist family there were many supporters of the old church including the Pilchers, the Houks, Laughridges, and Thomases, as well as many others. New windows were installed.

In 1916 Sunday School was again organized by J. E. Crist, along with his son Ottis and Ottis's wife Corda, all living in Floris at that time. Sunday School and preaching services were held for a few years, until World War I began in 1917, and many of the young men were called again into military service.

Joel E. Crist with some of the cement blocks he and a group of men used to build a new foundation under the church.

Ottis E. Crist, Joel's son, at age 16 in about 1894.

convention

Sunday Sept. 24, 1916 Mays Hill Mission Sunday school met at the usual time Juning by singing no 45-18. Scripture reading first 16 v, of the 22nd chapter of acts Prayer

Song no. 94        quarterly Lesson individual review of the read by Supt and school Classes took there respective places. Class report

| Class | Att. | Chap. | Offering |
|---|---|---|---|
| Class A | 3 | | 6 |
| Class B | 13 | 5 | 10 |
| Class C | 4 | 7 | 2 |
| Class D. | 9 | 7 | 6 |
| Teachers and Officers Pres | 4 | | |
| Total | 33 | 19 | 24 |

Record of Sunday School classes and lessons, 1916

## Mars Hill Church

My interest in the Mars Hill Church and Cemetery runs deep. My grandfather, Francis Niles, has been buried in the Mars Hill Cemetery for 99 years. He died January 20, 1909.

Francis Niles lived in the Floris area. He married Catherine Isabell Post and they had four children.

When my grandmother passed away in April of 1946, we wanted to bury her beside Grandpa. We could not do this because there was no road. The snow had melted and it rained a lot, so the hearse could not get to the cemetery. There was just a lane back to the cemetery at that time. So Grandma Niles is buried on a lot with my parents, Slim and Mable Niles, in the I.O.O.F. Cemetery in Bloomfield.

Soon after her death, my father went to the Davis County Board of Supervisors in Bloomfield to ask for a road to be built to the cemetery. Of course, they said no. But one of them, Jim Bish, sided with my dad. It was a fight for two years, but they finally did relent and built what is now the road to the cemetery and the church. Thanks to my father and the late Jim Bish, there is now a road to the cemetery.

I can remember, as a young teenager, my mother, my grandmother, and my great aunt, Abigail (Ab) Post all going to the Mars Hill June celebration. We took our picnic lunch and were there all day. We always sat on the bleachers between the fence and the church to hear the service. They opened the windows of the church, so we could hear. The church would be filled to capacity.

The pews were all polished and cleaned, the pulpit was nice and shiny, and the organ that sat in the corner on the stage made beautiful music. I don't know who played the organ, but the old hymns were loud and clear and beautiful.

During the year, the large registry book was left on the pulpit so those of us visiting the cemetery could sign and date our visit. I hope someone has that book.

Going to the Mars Hill Cemetery is one of the most inspiring times ever. It is so quiet and peaceful. The wind whispering through the trees, the birds singing, and a feeling of calm that comes over you while standing in the midst of what moments are left.

May God bless all of those who are still helping to save this historical place of serenity.
--Lucille (Niles) McConnell

A Living Legacy

Sunday school class, 1917

Sunday School class, 1918, outside the church. Corda Crist (in hat) is at left in the back row.

Sunday School class, 1917 At left is Marie Crist, later Mrs. Harley Hartwig.

## Mars Hill Church

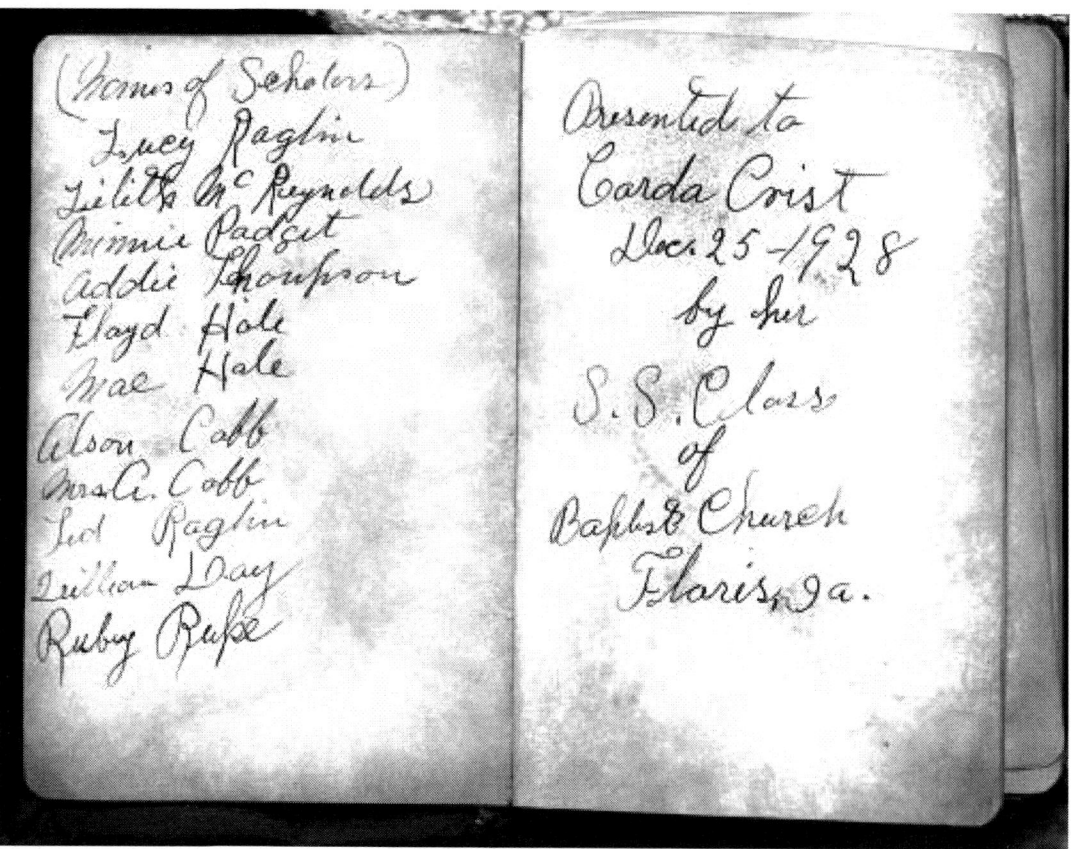

Bible presented to Corda Crist in 1928 by her Sunday school class at the Floris Baptist Church, after the Mars Hill Sunday school once more closed down. Class members are listed at left.

> One of my first memories of Mars Hill is going there to clean the graves of my grandparents in the spring. Dad would harness up the team of horses, hitch up the wagon, and put in shovels, rakes and bucket, then we as a family -- Dad, Mom, my brother and I -- would get in and off we would go. The distance was only about 1 1/2 miles, but the last 3/4 mile could hardly be called a road... If we cut across the fields, it was only about a mile. If it was a wet spring, there would be water holes and muddy stretches. Once there we would rake and clean off all the leaves and dead grass, and if the graves had sunken in, we would carry buckets of dirt to fill them in. We always visited the church and signed the book. Once inside, I remember the wooden pews, the organ, pulpit, wood stove and oval picture of Christ, the Good Shepherd, that hung on the wall. --*Benjamine Post (recalling 1947-48)*

# A Living Legacy

Photo by Michael W. Lemberger

## Mars Hill Church

### THE OLD LOG CHURCH
### By Pearl Rupe Harness

On an Iowa Hill, high above the fogs
Stands an old gray church men built of logs;
And there it has stood, over a hundred years
This old log church built by pioneers.

They chopped the logs and hewed them square
Laid them end on end as you see them there,
They morticed the corners to keep them in place
And chinked up the cracks to give them face.

This undated photograph shows a baptism held at Soap Creek, north of Floris.

Made of Clapboard roof, and a puncheon floor
And from native lumber they made a door,
It was finished and high on an Iowa hill,
Was a place for worship, and it stands there still.

They made the building good and strong,
And, as they worked, praised God in song;
There it has stood, and stands there still,
The old Log Church they named MARS HILL.

## Mars Hill Church

Lemberger Collection

A group of skiers enjoy the hillsides near Mars Hill Church in January, 1942.

Lemberger Collection

# A Living Legacy

Lemberger Collection

Lemberger Collection

Lemberger Collection

# Mars Hill Church

Lemberger Collection

Lemberger Collection

# A Living Legacy

Lemberger Collection

Lemberger Collection

## Mars Hill Church

**"STATEMENT"**

On this 26th day of _____ 1968, I, O. E. Crist of Eldon, Iowa, and only living Trustee of the Mars Hill Baptist church, lying in the South edge of Wapello County and 4mi. North West of Floris, Ia, and by the order of the Rules as laid down in years past, do at this time appoint the following persons to serve along with me as a board of Trustees.

Harry Thomas, Eldon, Iowa to serve as Chairman.
Mrs. Mary Martsching Thomas, Eldon, Iowa.   Mr. Emmet Humble, Floris, Iowa.
Any one of these may retire upon the request to the membership, and another appointed to fullfil the vacancy.

It is agreed between Harry Thomas, Mary Thomas, Emmet Humble and myself, that---Mrs. Marie Crist Hartwig be appointed to serve as a life-time member of the board.

Be it known that, no organization, group or Convention shall have or be given control over the church or its property without the full knowledge and consent of all of the members of the Board.

Be it known that---it shall remain a community church serving the community, its lands as a burrial ground, and a place of fellowship as was orriginally intended.

There is a fund set up in the First National Bank of Eldon, Iowa for the benefit of the upkeep of the building, anyone wishing to contribute to this fund for this cause may do so by leaving same at the Bank, or placing same in the hands of any one of the Trustee members.

Sworn to before me, Notary Public _____

---

Note:-by K. Marie Crist Hartwig, senior board member and daughter of Ottis E. Crist.

Ottis E. Crist spent 50 years in labor, along with his wife Corda until her death in 1951, in and around tha old church. He helped dig many a grave, made many repairs, cleaned, mowed. He and Corda organized the Sunday School, with the help of his Father J.E.Crist.
He served as School Superintendent and teacher. Mrs Crist taught classes, daughters Marie and Marvel played the old organ. Four others Florence Allen, Hubert and Olive were small and spent time at Sunday School.
Ottis as his friends knew him, spent many years as a board member, and was serving as such at his death in 1963.
It was a family project, and a labor of Love for and in the Lord!

# A Living Legacy

The Crist family carried on with upkeep and care of the church for many years. Ottis Crist's daughter, Marie Crist Hartwig, recalls that her father "spent 50 years in labor, along with his wife Corda until her death in 1951, in and around the old church. He helped dig many a grave, made many repairs, cleaned, mowed... He served as School Superintendent and teacher. Mrs. Crist taught classes, daughters Marie and Marvel played the old organ. Four others – Florence, Allen, Hubert, and Olive – were small and spent time at Sunday School. Ottis, as his friends knew him, spent many years as a board member, and was serving as such at his death in 1963."

Young folks grew up, married, and left. Families moved away, and so few remained that it was impossible to keep the services going. Again the old church was closed except upon special occasions.

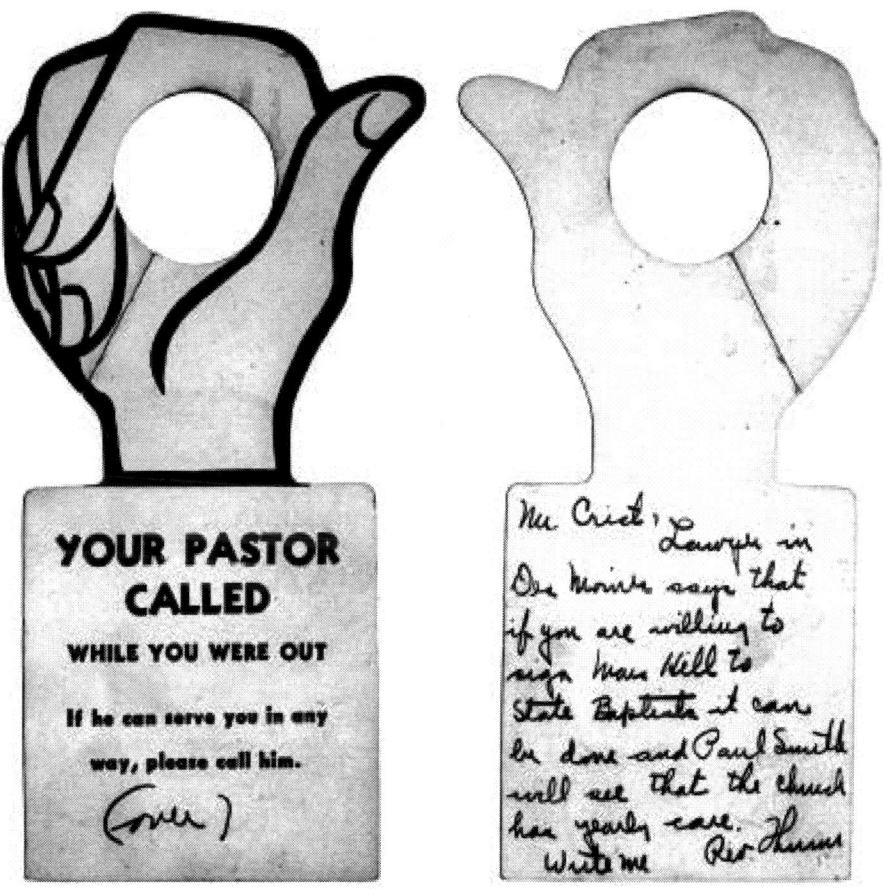

**Left and above: As Ottis Crist aged, he was concerned about the church he had tended for so many years. He made arrangements to name a new board to carry on, and looked into the possibility of passing the church on to an established group.**

## Mars Hill Church

## REUNIONS

In 1925, Mars Hill celebrated a pioneer reunion and picnic marking nearly 75 years since the founding of the congregation.

The first annual reunion was held in 1927, a custom which continues today.

Left to right: Ottis Crist, M. Grinstead, V. Pilcher, H. Stark, at 1925 reunion

# A Living Legacy

A local newspaper reported:

## 2,000 AT OLD LOG CHURCH

It was the spirit of the pioneer which ruled the 2,000 or more people who gathered at the historic old MARS HILL LOG CHURCH near Floris Sunday for a pioneers' reunion and picnic in 1925.
Homage to the pioneers who built that old log structure for the worship of God in what was then a wilderness, was the trend of the occasion, upon the hundreds of people who gathered there, was impressed deeply a realization of the sacrifices which their forefathers had made there, and the zeal with which they overcame obstacles to provide a place to worship their God.

## ATMOSPHERE THERE

There was a strange contrast in the occasion. To stand upon the knoll where the old log church is located and look upon the timberlands stretching faraway, and might think yet that the church stood in a frontier wilderness. The atmosphere was there. Yet it was but a short distance away – especially for the modern automobiles, which came by hundreds – to a densely peopled farm region and to modern city.
In a faltering voice, G. Monroe told how his father, S.A. Monroe, and Abraham Smock had supplied the logs for this church, built about 1855, 1856, or 1857. Others who spoke impressed upon the audience the devoutness of the pioneers who had laboriously hewn the huge logs of the old church from trees of the forest, hauled them to the crest of the hill, and there fitted them together to make a church.
Among those who paid their tribute to the pioneers were B.A. Carroll of Des Moines, Alex Miller of Washington, Milo Reno of Agency, Iowa and a number of other speakers.

**Left: An early guest book, not dated**

## Mars Hill Church

### HUNDREDS EXPECTED AT MARS HILL

MARS HILL CHURCH.

Floris.—Hundreds of persons are expected here Sunday for the annual homecoming and basket dinner at the Mars Hill church, two and one-half miles north of here Sunday. The above picture, taken this week, shows the church as it appears today. The log structure was built in 1856 and 1857 and is therefore marking its eightieth anniversary this year.

### MARS HILL; RALLY SITE

**PIONEERS OF FOUR COUNTIES INVITED TO REUNION AT HISTORIC CHURCH.**

A big pioneer reunion, embracing four counties, is being planned for July 26 at Mars Hill church, in the southern part of Wapello county, near the Davis county line. People from Wapello, Davis, Van Buren and Jefferson counties, and especially the old settlers, are invited.

Rev. J. A. Brown of Albia, pastor of the church, states that a program which will include addresses by prominent men of the state is being planned.

Mars Hill church is an especially fitting background for an occasion of this kind. It is claimed to be the oldest church in the state of Iowa where services are yet even occasionally held. It is also thought to be one of the oldest, if not the oldest, of any pioneer log structures remaining within Iowa.

The church was built in 1856, and during its long years of service many famous men have spoken there on religious, political and other missions.

The celebration July 26 will be a basket dinner and program. Everyone is invited to come. The location is four miles north of Floris. The road will be in good condition for the occasion, Rev. Mr. Brown states. The church is located just a few feet north of the Davis county line, which runs before the front door in the accom-

### "IOWA'S OLDEST"

Mars Hill church, the oldest church in Iowa still in use, and one of very few remaining log structures of pioneer origin in the state, will be the appropriate setting for an old settlers' reunion Sunday, July 26.

# A Living Legacy

MARS HILL REUNION LEADERS

GROUP AT MARS HILL SERVICES

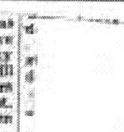

Left and above: News stories about the tenth Mars Hill Church reunion, in 1936.

## Mars Hill Church

left to right: Ed Brooks, Oliver Brooks, Bertha Brooks Kruson?, Ella Brooks Holcomb, 1946. Note the bus which may have brought people to the reunion.

Members of the church, pictured in 1966. left to right: Dewey Hancock, 82, T.K. Loring, 65, Ray Dearbourn, 78.

Hubert Joel Crist and his mother, Corda Mae (Brooks) Crist, August 1947

## A Living Legacy

left to right: Corda Mae (Brooks) Crist, Charles Taylor, Otis Crist, Ida Hawkins -- August 1947

left to right: Ottis Crist, Harley Hartwig, Charley Hartwig, Ott Oswalt

left to right: Olive Crist Gideon, Marvel Crist Brooks, Ottis Crist, Marie Crist Hardwig

## Mars Hill Church

The Mars Hill Baptist Church, a log building two and a half miles northwest of Floris, was completed in the fall of 1856, just 100 years ago.

An elderly couple stopped and asked how to find Mars Hill, and dad told them... he didn't think they would be able to drive there but he could take them to it in the horse and wagon. Of course my brother and I went also. I remember them looking around the grave yard at different tombstones and taking flash bulb pictures inside the church. When we got back to our house, they wanted to give dad some money but he wouldn't take it, so they ended up giving my brother and me a dollar each. Later after they did work on the road, several of us boys would ride our bikes to the church. There are only about two houses that I can remember still standing along the road from that time...  --Benjamine Post

left to right: Harry Holcomb, Gilbert Howk, Junior Holcomb.
Notice the sidewalk and gate, which also appear in the illustration above.

## MID-20th CENTURY

By 1956, a new roof was needed. A group of workers headed by Ottis E. Crist, then of Eldon, solicited money and work from those interested in the church, and a new roof was put on, plus other repairs were made to the outside of the building.

At about the same time, new roads were constructed by both the Wapello County supervisors and the Davis County supervisors to allow access to Mars Hill. A newspaper story announcing

left to right: not known, Charley Hartwig, Ottis Crist, not known.

Salem Iowa
Mar-18-71

Mrs Harley D. Hartwig
    Eldon Iowa

Dear Mrs Hartwig:-
    My daughter wrote Mr W Sinclair Venables about the Mars Hill Chapel. We were there one Sun P. M. last fall and was so pleased to see how the Historical Society had cleaned and repaired the chapel.
    We noticed different items had been donated in memory of people, except the organ, which we gave to the chapel in memory of our mother Mrs Martha Brown Wiedmeyer, in the summer of 1955.
Mrs Ethel Ensminger. Salem Iowa 52649.
Miss Martha Wiedmeyer, West Point Ill 62380
Mr William Russell Wiedmeyer 518 Orleans St. Keokuk Iowa.
    Martha Brown Wiedmeyer was the daughter of John G. Brown who is buried in the cemetry, also her mother Sarah who is buried in the front row by the tree. William, Samuel and Joseph are Mothers brothers Grandpa Brown was married three times so all the Brown's are our relatives.
    My Mother was borned in 1866 but went to work when she was sixteen, so we know no history of the chapel. We children thought maby you didnt know who donated the organ and stool which I see is gone.
            Resp Yours
            Mrs Ethel Ensminger
                Salem Iowa 52649.

## A Living Legacy

the construction said that for about 25 years before the roads were built, access to the church had been limited and visitors had to walk to the site.

A pump organ was donated in the summer of 1955 in memory of Mrs. Martha Brown Wiedmeyer, the daughter of John G. Brown who was buried in the cemetery, in the row of graves nearest the church. The organ, donated by Mrs. Wiedmeyer's children, had been purchased in 1907 from the Kimball Organ Co. of Quincy, Illinois, for $85. The organ was later removed from the church and is stored at the Wapello County Historical Society museum, along with the pulpit.

Pianist Dan Knight, seated at the organ.

## Mars Hill Church

**1954**

...ollowing people have made donations for repair of this old church.
...ese people we give our full appreciation, with their donation we
...been able to restore the beauty of the old church.

- . Sickels
- ...r Joxes
- A Fred Lutes
- ...Hubman
- ...e Wilburn
- . Wabbefield
- R. E. Brooks
- Slim Miles
- Mrs. Claud Finney
- Pearl Harness
- C. E. Warden
- Eldon Bank
- Wallace Campbell
- Hollice Moore
- Grant Thomas
- W. J. Harper
- Sid Crow
- Mrs Fred Lutes
- Ira Wilkerson
- Mr. & Mrs. E. L. Younkin
- Charley Box
- Frank Rulman
- Malvel Brooks
- Tom McHaddem
- Vern Houk
- Mrs. Blanch Thard
- ...ret Streeby
- D. E. Oliver
- Joe Rodesky
- James Peck
- C. D. Evens
- J. P. Lurghridge
- Lee Laughridge

- Charley Hartwig
- Ott Tubbel
- Floris township
- John C. Shepard
- Frank Rulman
- O. G. Jackson
- Charley Hemm
- Leona Blanchard
- Ray Waller
- Giff Campbell
- Tom Lynch
- C. E. Cubbage
- Arnold Laughridge
- Clarence Lambert
- F. F. Ryehke
- Mrs. C. E. Brooks
- Mrs. C. S. Pikerl
- Hales Shop
- S. E. Reno & sons
- Mabel Finney
- A. C. Downing
- Nora Kittel
- Leo Fitzgerles
- A. C. Movery
- Brout Harward
- Mr. And Mrs. Lee Stevenson
- H. L. McMillen
- Henry Olebfield
- Ralph Wakon
- Carl Thomas
- Dave Kirkindal
- Arnold Laughridge
- Mr. George Isreal

Harley Sloan

*G C Brown*
*M. H. Hartwig*

The following have donated their time and efforts to the repairing of th...
odd church. To them we are also grateful.

- Mr. & Mrs. Harry Thomas
- Vern Houk
- Herbert Crist
- Roy Orman
- Charles Hartwig
- Emmet Humbel
- Ray Waller & son
- Carl Thomas
- O. E. Crist

- Mr. John Shepard
- Millard Houk
- Glean Orman
- Harley Hartwig
- Frank Rulman
- Fred Lutes
- Tom Lynch
- Eligie Thomas

*Ray Orman*
*L. H. Batterson*

To the repairs made to this ...ple church we can thank Mr. O. E. Crist, wh...
with deterninitation to get ... old church back in order, went out and h...
a collection from all the pe... who were willing to donate. Mr. O. E.
Crist is t... ...ee of the ol... church, and I can say from the bottom of ...
heart ... ...lly the m n for the job.
If ... to ...iv ...o that this old church may be always
... give it ... O. E. Crist, Eldon, Iowa.

A 1954 listing of people who had made donations for the repair of "this old church"

# A Living Legacy

Interior of church, date unknown. Note the stove (left) and organ (right).

## Mars Hill Church

Choir practice, July 1965. The men are identified as Jr. McCarroll at the pulpit and Kenneth Derby sitting at the organ. Back row (left to right) Hank Glenn, John Noe, Richard Wilhoit, Albert Major. Front row (left to right) Bill Ollaughlin, Bernard Bohe, Don Wiley.

In 1963, Dr. Paul Smith, executive secretary of the Baptist State Convention of Iowa, said in an address at the church, "Mars Hill is the Mother Church of all Baptist Faiths West of the Mississippi."

In 1963 the Keokuk Township Boys 4-H Club planted spreading junipers. In the summer of 1968, Henry Gruwell and his son-in-law Leonard Fiedler re-nailed and painted the ceiling, whitewashed the walls and painted the floor.

### 1,790 Register At Old Church Near Floris

*June 1965*

FLORIS — Portage la Prairie, Manitoba, Canada and Bombay, India, appear as addresses of persons registering at the century-old Mars Hill Church northwest of Floris.

Some 1,790 names have been registered within the past year in the book kept on the old altar for that purpose. Iowa addresses appear most frequently with California next with people coming from throughout the nation.

The church is the original 26 by 28 foot building which was finished in 1856. Said to be the largest log structure ever to have been erected in the state, it is made of hand-hewn logs, mostly oak and walnut.

Within the past few years the church has been restored to it's original state as nearly as possible. It is maintained by a board of trustees and others who are interested in preserving antique landmarks.

Less than a year ago vandals upset and broke many of the tombstones in the adjoining cemetery. Most have been reset and restored where possible.

At present the church, church yard and cemetery have a well cared for look.

The annual reunion will be held in July.

*A Living Legacy*

## THE CHURCH ON MARS HILL
**By D. Y. Bevington**

High up on the crest of a hill stands a tree
That highlights a structure that's lovely to see –
A church, hewn of logs fitted tightly in place
Stands as a reminder of God's love and grace.

She sits dressed in white, in seclusion by day,
A silent reminder of another day,
The mid-1800s was when she began –
Just reading her story can make one feel grand.

Once vibrant with life, its place was assured
As folks miles around came to worship the Lord.
That church was the center of life in its day,
And it was a blessing to all down that way.

The years came and passed, and time took its toll,
And wars came and went to trouble its soul.
The children grew up to marry one day –
Most moved to some other place, far away.

Though founded on hope, they closed the church down –
The church on Mars Hill sits, devoid of all sound.
The log structure stands – it's one of a kind,
It's treasured by many who keep it in mind.

The call to the world from the church on Mars Hill
Is, "God is still calling," – He gives us the will
to HOPE and to WORSHIP, to SERVE and to PRAY,
To place faith in Jesus, the TRUTH, LIFE, and WAY.


(Reverend Bevington was repairing and cleaning the Mars Hill Church organ in 1989, when he wrote this poem.)

## Mars Hill Church

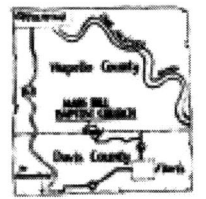

The Painting on the Cover

# Iowa Landmark Being Restored

By Frank Miller

At the north edge of Davis County, in the wooded hills of Lick Creek Township, stands an interesting Iowa landmark—The Mars Hill Baptist Church, pictured on today's cover. It is one of the largest log structures ever built in the state.

Among the earliest settlers who moved into Iowa and established farms along the Des Moines River were a number of Baptist families. The first thing they did after building their cabins was to establish a church. They formed a congregation that held services in their frontier homes until a church could be erected. In 1857 the building was started by volunteer labor of the congregation. Huge logs of oak and walnut were hewn square and the ends notched for morticing the corners. When completed the log church measured 26 feet wide by 28 feet long, with walls 10 feet high. Roof shingles and shake siding were fashioned by hand, and and huge stones were hauled from the Des Moines River for the fireplace. With the church completed, services were held every third Sunday of each month "with preaching the Saturday night before".

**HIDING PLACE FOR SLAVES**

The Civil War affected the church's history in several ways. Legend and "handed down history" say the church was used as a hiding place for slaves traveling the Underground Railroad. During the war about 35 men of the church left for service in the army, and after the war a number of the Baptist families of the area moved away. The remaining members joined with Baptists of the village of Floris to build a church closer to town, leaving the old one abandoned in the woods.

Recently steps have been taken to preserve the Mars Hill Church. Davis and Wapello Counties have opened roads to the site and a number of private citizens have become interested in restoration of the building. Leader of this restoration project is 78-year-old O. E. Crist, of Eldon. Mr. Crist's first recollection of the church was on a Sunday School hayride in the spring of 1896. Since then he and his family have visited the church often and have become interested in saving the old landmark.

**ORIGINAL LOGS BEING RETAINED**

With the help of neighbors and friends in the area he has been working to rebuild the decaying and weathered building. A new roof has been put on it, new siding on the gabled ends has been added. The original old logs have been kept in place but "re-chinked" with cement. Soon a new door will be put into place.

Restoring the Mars Hill Baptist Church not only saves a fine example of pioneer labor and craftsmanship but also preserves a reminder of the important part religion played in the lives of Iowa settlers a century ago.

ON A WINTER DAY this old log church stands lonely and deserted among the trees. This painting, like the one on the cover, and like the sketches below, is by Register Artist Frank Miller.

THE INTERIOR of the church, like the exterior, betokens its age. Backs of the sturdy benches still reveal initials carved by jackknives of a pioneer boyhood.

THE CRAFTSMEN of a century ago built well and strong. An Iowan from the neighborhood inspects the morticing of the heavy oak and walnut logs at one corner.

DES MOINES SUNDAY REGISTER—JANUARY 20, 1957—PAGE 5

Frank Miller, Pulitzer-Prize winning cartoonist for the Des Moines Register, visited Mars Hill and wrote an illustrated story about the 1957 renovation of the church. (The magazine cover he drew is on page 4.) Unfortunately, in the story, Miller moved Mars Hill into Davis County.

## A Living Legacy

### Keeping the record straight

*July 1968*

To the Editor of Courier, and anyone else in authority.

Re: Mars Hill Church.

QUOTE:

"Filed for record May 22, 1857, at 5 o'clock P.M.

Recorded May 29, 1857.—Peter Knox, Rec. by F. Hoddy, Dept.

Barbara Clark deed to Baptist Church—

For and in consideration of the Regard & Esteem I have for Christianity & benevolent institutions. I hereby convey to A. Smock, S. A. Monroe & A. Clark, the Trustees of the Missionary Baptist Church at Mars Hill and to their Successors in office the following tract of land & described by meets and Bounds as follows to-wit: Commencing at the South East corner of the South West quarter of the South East quarter of Section Thirty-Three (33) in Township Seventy-one (71) Range Thirteen West, thence North Thirteen rods and thence Due West Eighteen & a half rods thence due South Thirteen rods to South line of said Section thence East along Said Section along Said Section Line Eighteen & a half rods to the place of beginning in the State of Iowa & Wapello County to have and to hold the Same for the use of the said Baptist Church as long as they Shall continue the use of the Said Lot for a church Lot & Bury-ground. And Warrant the Title against app persons whosoever. In Testimony thereof I have hereunto set my hand and Seal This the 16th day of May A.D. 1857.

—Barbara Clark. (SEAL)

STATE OF IOWA
WAPELLO COUNTY/ SS

Personally appeared before the undersigned a Justice of the Peace in and for the County above named Barbara Clark to me personally known to be the person whose named is subscribed to the within deed as a party thereto & acknowledged she executed the Same as her own voluntary act & deed for the purposes therein contained. This 16 day of May, A.D. 1857."

END OF QUOTE.

What in ........ well, the name and interest of common sense and the purveyance of correct information, will it take to convince the Courier, and some other wiseacres, that Mars Hill (The Old Log Church) is in Wapello County?

Yes, I'm mad, and have been for a good many years, at the attempt of the Courier and others to give this church and cemetery to Davis County. Davis County has its Dunville, and a few other things, but by all that is good and legal, Wapello County has Mars Hill.

Let's keep the record straight,

—Pearl Rupe Harness

*Frank Miller wasn't the only one who was confused about the exact location of Mars Hill.*

## John F. Knight and the Amish Repair of Mars Hill Church:
### *An Experience in Multicultural Communications*

Somewhere in the late 1970s, when it became apparent that a few rotting logs at Mars Hill Church were in dire need of replacement, it was decided by the Board of Directors of Mars Hill Church that the most likely resource for getting replacement timbers would be the local Amish community. My father, John F. Knight, was the board member appointed to be "point man" for the project.

**Descendants of Barbra Clark, who donated the land where Mars Hill Church stands. Left to right: Mrs. Wilton Cornell, Arthur S. Taylor, Mrs. James Nickolas, all of California, when they visited Mars Hill in September 1974.**

---

Dad was selected because he had been a construction supervisor for Northwestern Bell Telephone Company. He was used to assessing projects, supervising contractors, and guiding projects along to their successful completion. He thought the job was going to be a straightforward repair project: have the appropriate timber cut at a local lumber mill, and hire workers from the local Amish community to do the repair work.

After consultation with local farmers who had friends in the Amish community, the name of an Amish gentleman whom we shall call M.K. was mentioned. M.K. had worked on several other cooperative projects involving Amish workers and local farmers, and it was the common consensus that M.K. would be the best man to "coordinate" the Amish side of the Mars Hill repair.

A Living Legacy

## Many Sign Register At Log Church

*July 16, 1971*

FLORIS. — Historic Mars Hill log church, four miles north of Floris, had 1,611 visitors during the past year.

Registrations are made in a ledger kept on the pulpit for that purpose. One hundred signed on Memorial Day alone.

Addresses include 46 cities outside of Iowa. Included were persons from Colorado, Texas, California, Nebraska, Florida, Missouri, Wyoming, Illinois, Minnesota, New York, Oregon, Arizona, Georgia, North and South Dakota, Arkansas, Oklahoma, Kansas and Canada.

## Laurie Raisbeck married at Mars Hill

*May 1970 - 24*

MRS. BAILEY

The 120-year-old Mars Hill Church north of Floris was chosen by Laurie Raisbeck for her wedding to G. W. Bailey. They were married at 2:30 p.m. by the Rev. Louis Wollenberg, minister of First Presbyterian Church.

Parents of the couple are W. P. Raisbeck of 1135 N. Court and Mr. and Mrs. G. W. Bailey of 830 Albia Road.

The attendants were Julie Benoodt and Kent Jackson.

Mr. and Mrs. Raisbeck were hosts at the reception at their home.

The couple will live in Iowa City where both are sophomores at the University of Iowa. She is employed at the K-Mart and he at the Union Bus Depot, both in Iowa City.

---

That's when the "fun" began.

"Coordination" took on a different connotation in the Amish community, which still used 1850's means of communication. "Modern" people take instant communication via phone and email for granted: a "modern" contractor would have contacted his workers by phone and arranged the entire repair in an afternoon. Amish communications moved at the speed of the U.S. Postal System, or horse and buggy, whichever was quicker. And, as Dad was soon to find out, Amish business customs moved at precisely the same speed as their communications.

A meeting between Dad and M.K. was arranged. M.K. decided that since the repair was outside the Amish community, a "special" repair team had to be organized. To do this, Dad shuttled M.K. and his family across Southern Iowa as M.K. met with other Amish farmers to discuss the weather, farming

## Mars Hill Church

### 1962
### Funds Sought For Mars Hill Repairs

FLORIS — During the annual reunion Sunday it is hoped to raise enough money for repair of the ceiling and restoration of the organ of Mars Hill Baptist Church.

The log church, 116 years old, is maintained by voluntary labor and donations.

Thousands of visitors register at the church annually. It can be reached by going north out of Floris, turning left at the first crossroad then taking the first road to the right.

Situated in hilly land, the church and adjoining cemetery are surrounded by dense timber and have much the appearance they must have had at the time of origin, except for the graveled road leading past them.

A basket dinner at noon will be followed by a song and praise service beginning at 2 o'clock. The Rev. John Falconer of the Eldon Baptist Church will be the afternoon speaker.

---

problems, church issues, family news, and, occasionally, specifics about the Mars Hill Church repair, how it might best be accomplished, who might be willing to help, and when they might be available.

There was a lot to discuss. The old, decaying logs were slightly irregular. They had been felled and trimmed to shape by hand, after all, morticed by hand, and had settled into their current position amid the other logs in the walls of Mars Hill Church after over a century of wear and tear. Should the new logs be cut and shaped by hand, as the original logs were? Could they be cut at the local sawmill then shaped by hand? Or should they be sawn at the mill and inserted "as is"? How "green" could the new logs be? Would "green" lots "set" properly? How would the new logs withstand the weight of the building above them?

On top of it all, most of the discussion between Amish was in "old German."

A discussion at one farm would often inspire a visit to yet another farm and another "consultation" between M.K. and another Amish expert, who would give yet another opinion on how best to do the work. This would, of course, mean that whenever there was a disagreement as to what was to be done and how best to do it, consensus had to be established, yet again, and all of the previous consultees had to be revisited. Other Amish families soon began accompanying M.K. and Dad on their trips between farms, using the opportunity to visit family members and friends.

Dad went weeks, then months, with nothing but "discussion" to show for his trips between Amish farms.

## A Living Legacy

Dad figured out, after more than a little frustration, that something was going wrong. He spoke with his farmer friends who had experience with Amish culture. His friends told him he needed to set specific deadlines for the completion of the Mars Hill project, because if he didn't, these "discussions" might continue indefinitely.

Dad considered the task at hand, then set what he thought might be a fair timeline for completion of the project. After a few complaints from M.K. things finally began to progress in a slow but substantial way from discussion to actual work.

Logs were measured, and the millwork for the replacement logs was completed. Because the logs were sawn instead of rough-hewn by hand, as the original logs were, they stood out a little from the originals. Eventually the work was completed in a way that satisfied everyone's expectations. The quality of the repair and the craftsmanship involved was beyond reproach. M.K. got a summer's worth of visiting family and friends in a chauffeured, air conditioned automobile. Dad got a lesson in patience and perseverance.

And the walls of Mars Hill Church were strong once again.

-- *Dan Knight*

## Mars Hill Church

Photo by Michael W. Lemberger

Firmly embedded in my early memories are the many treks to a place called Mars Hill. My earliest recollection is as a child of six or seven in the mid-1940s... Daddy only drove about fifteen miles an hour, so it took a while to get to Mars Hill. Daddy had his own way to get there. We went out Rabbit Run Road, out over Monkey Mountain and finally to the Floris Road. We anxiously waited as we came over the last hill and there on the horizon were the three majestic pine trees that towered above the tree line, and we knew we were almost to our destination.

We drove to the trail that meandered alongside the south

# A Living Legacy

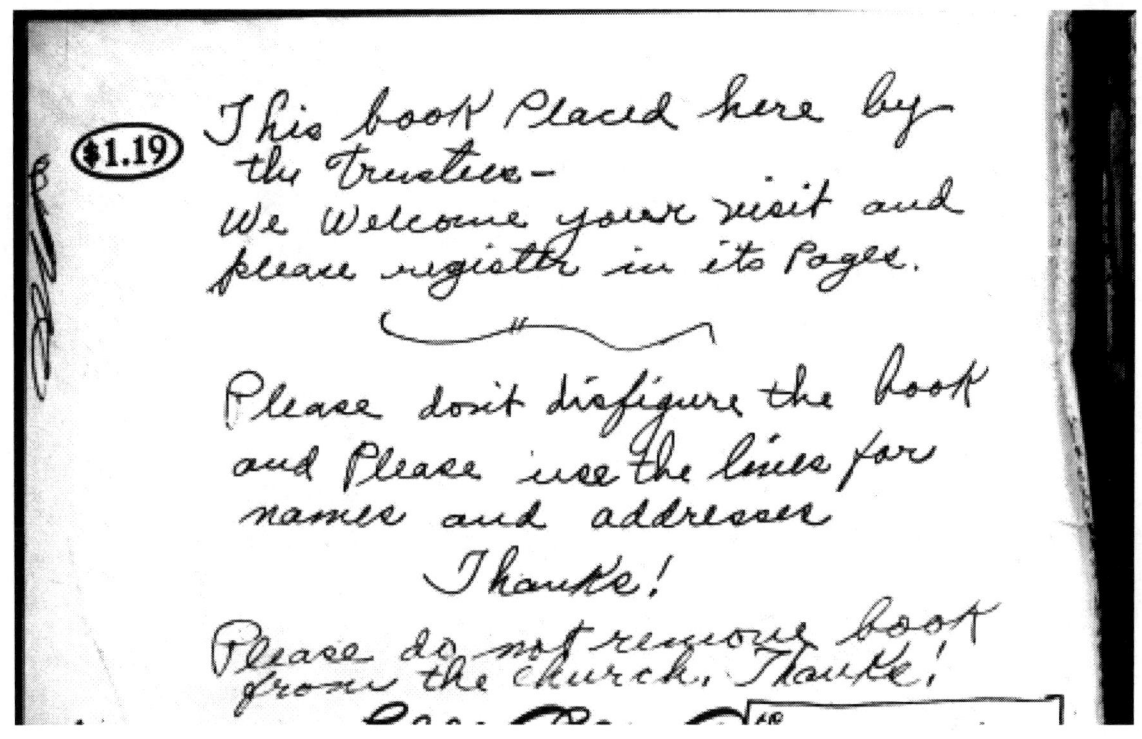

**Guest books, above and above left.**

side of the creek. I remember moving fallen limbs from the trail. Sometimes the trail was just not passable and we would end up walking into the church but we always got there... I was probably about eight years old when I played my first pump organ solo with my mom and dad as my audience...

We always looked forward to getting inside the church. Mars Hill had its own smell. It was a smoky old wood and pine smell. There was no vandalism. The kerosene lamp, the pulpit, the guest book and the pictures on the wall were all there...

We went there for annual reunions, when we had out of town guests and when we needed to get away... In the early 60s, my sister-in-law, Nancy Yenger, and I were out riding in the country and we stopped at Mars Hill. I played the old organ and we sang any hymns out of the old hymnals. Everything was still intact. I remember many annual meetings and sometimes leading the singing... Mars Hill is in my blood. I was raised on the history and mystique of the place. I am so glad it has been rebuilt for my grandchildren and future descendants to enjoy.

–Sue Yenger

# Mars Hill Church

In 1969 the Iowa Chapter of the Daughters of American Colonists presented the church with a bronze plaque, honoring it as the "Oldest Log Church Still In Occupancy In The United States." The plaque was accepted on behalf of the church by Mrs. Marie Crist Hartwig.

Marie Crist Hartwig

## Our readers write...
## Mars Hill in Iowa

Editor, the Courier:

Church bells ringing in the town,
  Men in freshly-blackened shoes,
Wives in silk or velvet gowns,
  Children filling up the pews;

The choir singing in the loft,
  Every head bowed low in prayer,
The preacher uttered blessings, soft,
  It seemed God, too, was there.

Outside town among the hills
  There was no house of prayer.
Music made by tinkling rills
  Was proof that God was there.

Said Barbara Clark, "This will not do!
  I well can spare the land,
And men and boys will chop and hew
  Stout logs for a church to stand.

Where generations yet unborn
  Shall gather with their heirs,
On this hill that looks forlorn,
  To sing and offer prayers."

Thus, in eighteen fifty-one
  Barbara Clark gave up her land.
The needful work, with zest, was done,
  By a zealous, prayerful band.

Though there was no bell to ring,
  Folks went there to shout and pray;
Never a vested choir to sing;
  Voices praised on the Sabbath day.

In Mars Hill church, they fill each pew,
  As childrens' children worship, free,
The words of Barbara Clark can be true,
  In nineteen hundred seventy-two.

        Pearl Rupe Harness,
        2331 N. Court Street

*Hapells-Davis Co Line 1971*

A Living Legacy

## 'Oldest log church' plaque presented

The Iowa chapter of the Daughters of American Colonists has presented a bronze plaque to the board of the Mars Hill log church, reading "Oldest log church still in occupancy in the United States." Dates on the plaque are 1850-1969. Positioning the plaque with a paper "rubbing" taken from it are Mrs. Paul Shaffer, left, state regent of the DAC, and Mrs. Harley Hartwig of Eldon, chairman of the board of trustees of the Mars Hill Church. Mrs. Shaffer is executive director of Caravan Trails Girl Scout Council. Other trustees of the church are Mr. and Mrs. Harry Thomas of Eldon, Eugene Orman of Bloomfield, and Donald Pilcher of Washington, Iowa, a new member. The annual basket dinner was at the church Sunday and the afternoon speaker was the Rev. Ralph Edgerly of Floris. (Courier photo by Loree Roach).

# Mars Hill Church

## A Living Legacy

Mars Hill was featured on the magazine of the Iowa AAA (American Automobile Association) magazine in 1973.

Bill and I both have Great-Grandparents and I also have Great-Great-Grandparents buried at Mars Hill. Have reset the stones so many times because of vandals. We also have other family members buried there.

I remember as a child what a treat to go for a "Sunday Drive" and go to Mars Hill. I was allowed to, very carefully, print my name in the visitors book. [I] remember Grandma and my Mom and Dad walking through the cemetery telling of stories about the family. (How I wish I had listened closer.)

I am interested in genealogy and have traced mine and Bill's family. How great will be the Family Reunion when we again meet our loved ones, and the greatest to meet Jesus!

---*Phyllis Thomas*

## Mars Hill Church

> When a church houses a congregation, it becomes a part of the worship. Its altar is the most important place ... to the people who come to sing and pray and listen. Its roof resounds with the high notes and the snappy choruses of the revival-type hymns and its windows sometimes rattle with the oratory of a preacher who has taken seriously the Apostle Paul's instruction to teach "and exhort." Its roof shelters in time of storm and wards off the sun's rays in time of heat... When the building outlives its usefulness ... it houses the hearts and souls and thoughts of its former members. As the years pass it becomes even more sacred in its role of the house of God ... The children who learn their first lessons about God remember the atmosphere and the surroundings where they were taught as well as the lessons ... So the church of their youth becomes more precious as time dims the memories and takes away what they learned yesterday, while bringing into clearer focus what they learned long ago ... This explains the charm of the Mars Hill Church...
> – *Loree Roach, "The Charm of the Mars Hill Church"*
> *Ottumwa Courier, July 20, 1966*

**Worship service, 1966**

Photo by Loree Roach

A Living Legacy

United States Department of the Interior

NATIONAL PARK SERVICE
WASHINGTON, D.C. 20240

IN REPLY REFER TO:

The Director of the National Park Service

Ronald H. Walker

is pleased to inform you that the historic property listed on the enclosed sheet has been nominated by the State Historic Preservation Officer responsible for your State's implementation of the National Historic Preservation Act of 1966, P.L. 89-665 (80 Stat. 915), as amended. It has accordingly been entered in the National Register of Historic Places. A leaflet explaining the National Register is enclosed for your information and convenience.

Enclosures

### Mars Hill in National Register

The Mars Hill Church and cemetery north of Floris is included in the National Register of Historic Places. Harry Thomas, chairman of the board of trustees, has received the Congressional Certification for placement from Elisabeth Foxley, architectural historian.

The log church in a country setting is thought to be one of the largest single room log buildings in Iowa. All logs are original but new flooring was installed in 1901, a new foundation in 1915, and a new roof in 1966. The maple and walnut logs measure 26 or 28 feet long and some are 16 inches in width and eight inches thick.

A few of the original pews remain inside.

Built in 1857 by a Baptist community, the church is considered interdenominational and attracts visitors. The church is on a hill surrounded by pine trees.

An annual dinner is held there each summer and occasional weddings...

On September 13, 1974, Mars Hill was entered into the State of Iowa Register of Historic Places. On Sept. 24, 1974, Mars Hill Church was placed on the National Register of Historic Places.

# Mars Hill Church

**The church as it appeared in 1976**

Photos by Michael W. Lemberger

# A Living Legacy

Photo by Michael W. Lemberger

Photo by Michael W. Lemberger

## Mars Hill Church

Photo by Michael W. Lemberger

Pat Weeks and Richard Blew

Photo by Michael W. Lemberger

## A Living Legacy

### IOWA'S OLDEST CHURCH
### MARS HILL
**By Edna M. Shaw**

It is a small white slabbed
    church
Where all is quiet and still
And surrounded by giant oaks
Located on top of MARS HILL.

It has a little wooden cross
That bedecks its gable
And built to let the people know
It was theirs to attend when able.

It has a few pegged-wood pews
That were made to seat the
    people
And built so many years ago
This church that has no steeple.

Photo by Michael W. Lemberger

It once had a minister
Who on Sunday made his way
With the help of horse and buggy
To preach a text that day.

It once was a lively church
And had many a bride and groom
To repeat their wedding vows
In the one little room.

And there a little organ stands
And tiny pulpit, too
By the side of a pot-bellied stove
Our forefathers built for you.

And now this little country church
Is bare for want of man
And it's been preserved for all to see
If ever you are at hand.

## Mars Hill Church

REGISTER PHOTO BY DAVID PETERSON

### Carrying on a tradition

The annual gathering at the 135-year-old Mars Hill log church near Floris was held Sunday. Helping to provide the violin and harmonica music were, from left, Albert Coop of Albia and Marie Brooks and Captain John Smith, both from Ottumwa. Recent acts of vandalism at the church failed to put a damper on activities, which included a basket lunch

Anna Laughridge Pottorff

This pew, in an Ottumwa-area home, is thought to have come from Mars Hill.

# A Living Legacy

Photo by Michael W. Lemberger

left to right: Edith (Orman) Crist, Joel Crist, Carol Ann (Crist) Hoffman, Colleen (Hoffman) Baird, Brian Hoffman, Douglas Hoffman (back). Inside Mars Hill Church, about 1980.

# Mars Hill Church

Photo by Michael W. Lemberger

Photo by Michael W. Lemberger

A Living Legacy
# Mars Hill in new Iowa book

"MARS HILL BAPTIST CHURCH — FLORIS, IOWA"

William J. Wagner featured Mars Hill in his book, "Sixty Sketches of Iowa's Past and Present" (above) in 1967.

Kimberlee Ann Baird in the church on her fourth birthday, July 10, 1997

Mars Hill Church

Photo by Michael W. Lemberger

Left: Donna Smithhart reads minutes at an annual meeting as her husband Les looks on. Right: Jessica Kurtz sings at an annual meeting.

## A Living Legacy

**Pen and ink drawing by Bob Baughman**

Artist P. Buckley Moss released a limited edition print featuring Mars Hill Church, called "Pioneer Church", in 1991.

Installing a new sign outside the church, 2003.

# A Living Legacy

A group of Iowans on the Iowa "Eye to Eye" bus tour across the state stopped at Mars Hill for a worship service in 1995.

## Mars Hill Church

Todd Smithhart and Melinda Swanson were married at Mars Hill on June 6, 2004 -- the last wedding in the church before the 2006 fire.

Don Blew provides music for the Smithhart-Swanson wedding

A Living Legacy

Paul Frederickson (left) and Lois Frederickson, speakers at the
2005 annual reunion -- the last held in the church before the fire

Loading the organ up to deliver it to the Wapello County Historical Society.
At right is Rev. Dave Albert, pastor of the Living Hope Bible Church in Eldon,
the speaker at the 1998 annual meeting.

## Mars Hill Church

Lemberger Collection

The sentinel pine tree which towers above Mars Hill Cemetery is visible for miles. This photo was taken in 1942.

A Living Legacy

# MARS HILL CEMETERY

Since the first burial on the site, that of four-year-old John Clark in 1846, more than 250 people are believed to have been buried in Mars Hill Cemetery.

Isolated as it is, the cemetery has been an inviting target for vandals -- but time, weather, and tree roots have also caused damage to tombstones over the years. Volunteer workers have dug up, uncovered, straightened, cleaned, and repaired tombstones. Many of the stones pictured here as damaged have since been restored.

Photo by Michael W. Lemberger

Mars Hill Church

## List of Known Burials and Grave Markers at Mars Hill Cemetery

This alphabetical listing of known burials and markers is complete through early 2008. It has been compiled from a survey of stones and markers in the cemetery, then augmented with records of the cemetery, church, county, state, WPA, and families. Records are not always clear or complete; spellings vary. This is the best information available at this time.

Some burials may have been unrecorded.

**Anderson, Phebe Ella.** age 18y 2m 5d, died 7/15/1880. daughter of James & M. G. Anderson.

**Aulger, John.** age 60y 5m 11d, died 8/11/1872.

**Aulger, Mary.** age 62y. wife of John Aulger.

**Baird, Charles P.** age 38y 11m 29d, died 6/10/1884. born Ohio husband of Lucy ?, 6th Independent Battery, Ohio Light Artillery, Civil War.

**Baird, Willis E.** died 3/9/1871. son of Charles W. & M. ? Baird.

**Berry, John.** age 52y 2m 3d, died 4/12/1876. CO B 30th IA Infantry, Civil War.

**Berry, Joseph.** age 12y 5m 9d, died 4/21/1880. son of John & Lucy C. ? Berry.

Photo by Michael W. Lemberger

## A Living Legacy

**Beschje, Anna ??** age 59y 10m 17d, died 9/8/1878.

**Billhymer, Sarah Jane.** born 2/21/1806, died 2/21/1896. wife of E. G. Billyhymer. daughter of Greenville & Hannah Deckard Hale.

**Brooks, Emma.** age 8y, died 11/16/1887. daughter of Anson Brooks & Mary Patience Thomas Brooks.

**Brooks, Mary Patience.** age 27y 10m 2d, died 11/15/1887. wife of Anson. daughter of Benjamin Thomas & Mary Eggers Willis Thomas.

**Brown, Bessie.** born 1868, died 1934. wife of William W. Brown.

**Brown, Elizabeth.** age 3y 5m 12d, died 1/16/1868. daughter of John Gottlieb & Sarah Fiedler Brown.

Photo by Michael W. Lemberger

**Brown, Frederick E.** age 2m 4d, died 4/10/1880. son of S. G. & M. E.? Brown.

**Brown, Johanna.** age 40y 3m 9d, died 3/12/1861. wife of G. Brown.

**Brown, John.** age 2m 4d, died 4/10/1880. son of S. G. & M. E. ? Brown.

**Brown, John G.** age 26y 3m 21d, died 1/22/1882. son of J. G. & J. C.? Brown.

**Brown, John Godley.** born 8/23/1820, died 2/8/1905. 1st wife was Hannah Brown, 2nd wife was Sarah Fiedler (born Prussia).

**Brown, Joseph B.** born 1881, died 1960. son of John G. & Sarah Fiedler Brown.

**Brown, Samuel O.** born 1876, died 1947. son of John G. & Sarah Fiedler Brown.

## Mars Hill Church

Lemberger Collection

**Brown, Sarah.** age 39y 5m 29d, died 7/7/1868. 1st husband was John Newport, 2nd husband was John Gottlieb Brown. daughter of Johannes & Susannah Shreck Fiedler II.

**Brown, William W.** born 1859, died 1934. husband of Bessie. son of John Gottlieb & Sarah Fiedler Brown.

**Bryant, Lydia Ella.** age 21y, died 10/2/1871. wife of A. J. Bryant.

**Buchanan, Samuel.** age 87y 3m, died 1/18/1898. 1st wife was Sarah Toller (1898) 2nd wife was Linda or Lucinda Shaw (Ottumwa Cemetery). Body was moved 11/16/1917 to Ottumwa Cemetery. (Record Book 2 Page 512 Lot 56-57) CO D 15th IA Infantry, Civil War.

**Buchanan, Sarah.** age 65y, died 8/22/1865. 1st wife of Samuel E. Buchanan, daughter of ? Toller. born KY

**Campbell, Harold O.** died 3/2/1877. son of John C. & H. E. ? Campbell.

**Campbell, James M.** age 24 d, died 11/23/1878. son of John C. & H. E. ? Campbell.

**Cassill, Bertha.** 8/23/1907, 10/14/1987. 1st husband was ? Hopwood; 2nd husband was Herman Cassill. daughter of James Monroe & Eliza Matilda Foster Parker.

# A Living Legacy

**Cassill, Herman D.**   born 3/10/1909, died 1/16/1979. husband of Bertha Parker. son of Thomas & Mintie Russell Cassill.

**Clark, James C.**   age 26y 8m 10d, died 4/15/1854. husband of Mary Gillho. son of Thomas & Barbara Kees Clark. Died from cholera. Buried on Clark farm which became Mars Hill Cemetery.

**Clark, John.**   age 4y 7m 6d, died 10/12/1846. son of Thomas & Barbara Kees Clark. First known burial at the site which became Mars Hill Cemetery.

**Clark, Mina E.**   age 1y 1m 11d, died 4/5/1869. daughter of Andrew J. & Rachel C. Seeburn Clark.

**Clark, Thomas W.**   age 1y 6m 1d, died 1/2/1862. son of Andrew J. & Rachel C. Seeburn Clark.

**Clark, William W.**   age 2y 9m 5d, died 4/12/1851. son of James & Mary Gillho Clark.

**Crandall, Amanda.**   age 66y, died 8/18/1880. wife of Horace Crandall. born Ohio.

**Crandall, Horace S.**   age 7/24/1819, died 10/29/1864. husband of Amanda Rambo. son of Hampton Lillibridge & Freelove Butler Crandall. born Middlebury N. Y., Wyoming County. Died while on furlough., CO I 1st IA Cavalry, Civil War.

Photo by Michael W. Lemberger

## Mars Hill Church

Lemberger Collection

**Croft, William N.** born 12/20/1853, died 5/6/1909. husband of Elizabeth Hamilton. son of George Croft. born VA.

**Crook, Charles J.** born 1872, died 1955. (Campbell Funeral Home Marker).

**Crouse, Margaret L.** born 11/6/1932, died 7/15/1978. daughter of Arthur M. & Bessie McMath Post (Johnson Funeral Home Marker).

**Darneille, Charles F.** born 6/25/1856, died 3/22/1923. husband of Sara Anise. son of Thomas & Nancy Benson Darnielle, born MO.

**Darneille, Sara Anise.** born 12/12/1877, died 8/22/1962. wife of Charles Darnielle. daughter of Wm. & Elizabeth Owens Houk.

**Darneille, Tommie.** born 3/15/1916, died 11/30/1918. son of Charles F. & Sara Anise Houk Darnielle.

**Dommer, Margaret Jane.** born 3/22/1936, died 6/4/2000. wife of Wilford Dommer (divorced). daughter of Richard D. & Minnie Ruth Waller Donaldson.

# A Living Legacy

**Dommer, Meshell L.**   born 3/18/1963, died 3/18/1963. son of R. Wilford & Margaret Donaldson Dommer.

**Donaldson, Cora C.**   born 1869, died 1884. daughter of John P. & Susan Emeline Smock Donaldson.

**Donaldson, Edmund S.**   born 1873, died 1873. son of John P. & Susan Emeline Smock Donaldson (2 stones).

**Donaldson, Eliza.**   age 24 y, died April 1881. Wapello County Death Book 1 Page 19.

**Donaldson, Homer P.**   died 1879.

**Donaldson, John P.**   born 8/14/1842, died 1/7/1920. Serg. Co L 4th PA Cavalry, Civil War. Medal of Honor recipient. born Butler County, PA.

**Donaldson, Keith E.**   born 1924, died 1/20/1982. son of Richard & Ruth Waller Donaldson.

**Donaldson, Laura Livonia.**   born 5/18/1863, died 1/1/1960. wife of Richard Donaldson, daughter of James & Margaret Cumrina Houston.

**Donaldson, Mary D.**   age 74y 4m 4d, died 4/16/1890. wife of Milton Donaldson.

**Donaldson, Milton.**   born 1852, died 1926. husband of Mary D. ? born PA.

**Donaldson, Minnie Ruth.**   born 8/20/1907, died 9/15/1956. wife of Richard Donaldson, daughter of Joe & Dora Garretson Waller.

**Donaldson, Richard.**   born 1903, died 1978. husband of Ruth Waller. son of Milton & Laura Houston Donaldson.

**Donaldson, Sarah E.**   born 1871, died 1891.

**Donaldson, Sarah E.**   age 28y, died 3/4/1881. wife of H. or M. ? Donaldson.

**Donaldson, Susan Emeline.**   born 10/16/1852, died 8/17/1911. wife of John P. Donaldson. daughter of Abraham & Sarah Catherine Monroe Smock.

**Duffield, Barbara.**   age 71y, died 1/2/1877. wife of William D. Duffield.

**Duffield, Edmund.**   age 32y 5m 1d, died 9/15/1869. born 4/14/1837 in Steubinville, Ohio. son of Wm. & Barbara Rupe Duffield. CO E 3rd IA Cavalry, Civil War.

**Duffield, William.**   age 19y 10m 28d, died 11/23/1861. son of William D. & Barbara Rupe Duffield.

**Duffield, William D.**   age 89y 4m 14d, died 9/24/1887.

## Mars Hill Church

**Dunning, Georgia Ann.** age 33y 1m, died 8/16/1877. wife of John Wesley Dunning. daughter of Alexander & Anna ? Weddle.

**Dunning, John Wesley.** born 1871, died 1937. husband of Georgia A. Weddle (Johnson Funeral Home Marker).

**Dunning, Lulu.** Infant. daughter of James & Clara Garretson Dunning.

**Dunning, Sarah A.** age 28y 5m 11d. wife of ? Dunning.

**Dunning Children.** (stone located between Dunnings & Pilchers.)

**England, David S.** age 11y 5m 19d, died 11/8/1878. son of H. S. England & M. J.

**Fairburn, James T.** age 5y 7m 1d, died 7/27/1869. son of Moses & S. ? Fairburn.

Photo by Michael W. Lemberger

**Fairburn, Moses.** age 68y 8d, died 7/1/1871.

**Fitzgerald, Elizabeth.** born 1863, died 1922. wife of Samuel C. Fitzgerald.

**Fitzgerald, Samuel C.** born 1861, died 1939.

**Garrison, Addison A.** born 12/22/1830, died 12/28/1910. husband of Elizabeth McLain. son of Samuel S. & ? ? Garrison Wapello County Death Book born IL.

**Gordon, Charles.** born 8/21/1827, died 5/26/1909. husband of Mary Gallagher. born Ireland, came to U.S. 1855 from Derry, Ireland.

**Gordon, Mary.** born 3/20/1835, died 9/8/1921. wife of Charles Gordon.

**Hale, Catherine.** age 33y ,died 10/23/1853. wife of Wm. Hale. Copied from 1940 book WPA records.

**Hale, Emily.** age 54y 10d, died 3/7/1893. wife of John Hale.

Lemberger Collection

**Hale, Greenville.** age 78y 5m 2d, died 7/2/1898. husband of Hannah Deckard. CO E 36th IA Infantry, Civil War.

**Hale, Hannah.** age 70y, died 2/7/1894. wife of Greenville Hale. daughter of ? Deckard.

**Hale, Harold W.** born 7/27/1896, died 11/5/1908.

**Hale, Hiram.** age 34y, died 7/9/1872.

**Hale, Hiram.** age 73y 3m 27d, died 9/21/1898. husband of Mary A. ? CO E 36th IA Infantry, Civil War.

**Hale, John Jr.** age 34y 4m 2d, died 7/9/1872. husband of Emily Rhyme. born in Jackson County, Ohio. CO E 36th IA Infantry, Civil War.

**Hale, Mary A.** died 8/6/1905. wife of Hiram Hale.

**Hale, William B.** age 25y 10m, died 9/21/1872. husband of Catherine ? son of Grand M. & ?? Hale.

**Hamilton, William F.** age 50y 2m, died 10/31/1868. 3rd Pennsylvania Heavy Artillery. Civil War. Born IN.

## Mars Hill Church

Photo by Michael W. Lemberger

Photo by Michael W. Lemberger

**Hancock, Infant.** died 3/19/1908. son of F. D. & O. M. ? Hancock.

**Hancock, Laura M.** (no information)

**Hancock, Rufus.** born 1880, died 1950.

**Hand, Charles S.** age 6y 20d, died 8/25/1866. son of James A. & Hannah J. ? Hand.

**Hand, Hannah J.** age 30y 10m 22d, died 11/23/1870. wife of James A. Hand.

**Hand, James A.** age 50y 10d, died 6/2/1879.

**Hand, Sidney C.** age 1y 2m 6d, died 10/9/1870. son of James A. & Hannah J. ? Hand.

**Hand, Walter D.** age 2y 18d, died 6/24/1865. son of James A. & Hannah J. ? Hand.

**Hanmer, Mary F.** age 1y 7m 17d. died 7/26/1870. daughter of William H. & Susannah E. Slaught Hanmer.

**Hanmer, William H.** age 69y 1m 18d, died 1/31/1872. husband of Susannah E. Slaught.

## Mars Hill Church

**Harness, Gerald Arlett.** born 7/3/1911, died 11/28/1913. son of Giddeon Ralph & Pearl Rupe Harness.

**Harness, Susanna.** age 79y, died 4/7/1905.

**Harness, Mrs James.** age 17y 5m 27d, died 11/7/1905. wife of James Harness, daughter of John Pilcher.

**Harper, Danny Lee.** born 3/23/1955, died 5/23/1978. son of Linn & Deloris Nickell Harper.

**Harper, Deloris W.** born 1918. wife of Linn Harper.

**Harper, Linn D.** born 8/21/1901, died 10/16/1984. husband of Deloris W. Nickell. son of Ernest Harper & Olive Murphy.

**Hartwig, Infant.** Infant child of Charles & Paula A. ? Hartwig.

**Hartwig, Paula A.** born 6/19/1894, died 6/22/1922. wife of Charles Hartwig.

**Harwood, Jerusha Ann.** age 2y 3m 9d, died 11/1/1862. daughter of G. & N. ? Harwood.

**Harwood, Joseph.** age 16y 7m, died 7/22/1859. repaired stone.

**Hatch, Thomas Benjamin.** age 28y, died 5/7/1871. son of G. H. Hatch stepson of Andrew Martin, born 1843 in Ohio, CO B 7th IA Infantry, Civil War.

**Heady, William Harold.** born 7/9/1896, died 11/5/1898. son of Ullysses S. & Minnie O.? Heady.

**Heady Infant.** born 8/6/1893, died 8/8/1893. son of Ullysses S. & Minnie O. ? Heady.

**Heady, Mildred.** born 11/18/1906, died 12/3/1906. daughter of Ullysses S. & Minnie O. ? Heady

**Heady, Raymond.** born 6/27/1901, died 7/4/1901. son of Ullysses S. & Minnie O. ? Heady.

**Hitt, Halstead.** born 9/29/1821, died 6/7/1897. husband of F. Chesley Hitt.

**Hopwood, Anna M.** born 6/8/1926.

**Hopwood, Gary C.** born 2/12/1950, died 7/4/2000. husband of Carol Comer. son of James Clayton & Anna Marie Sullivan Hopwood. WW II U. S. Navy. (Reese Funeral Home Marker).

**Hopwood, Harry Milton.** born 4/22/1928, died 2/10/1967. son of Harry & Bertha Parker Herman Hopwood, WW II.

# A Living Legacy

Photo by Michael W. Lemberger

**Hopwood, James Clayton.** born 2/19/1925, died 5/17/1991. husband of Anna Marie Sullivan. son of Cloyd & Bertha Parker Hopwood. WW II Navy.

**Houk Infant.** died 7/4/1933. daughter of Vern S. & Ruby N. Richards Houk.

**Houk Infant.** died 4/19/1944. son of Vern S. & Ruby N. Richards Houk.

**Houston, James F.** born 1839, died 4/20/1896. born in Van Buren Co. died Davis Co. IA.

**Howard, Alvis.** age 38y 9m 18d, died 12/15/1901. (Death book 2 page 222).

**Howell, Addie M.** age 25y 10m 26d, died 4/27/1903. wife of Newton R. Howell.

**Howell, Newton R.** born 1873, died 1931. husband of Addie M. ?

**Hymer, Sarah J.** age 81y, died 2/21/1896. wife of E. G. Hymer.

**Jessop, Elsie Virginia.** born 2/16/1913, died 3/31/1934. daughter of ? Jessop & Maggie Sutton or Maggie Wake ? (Alexander Funeral Home Marker).

**Jessop, Gregg.** born 3/20/1938, died 3/20/1938. son of Grant & Marvelle Smith Jessop.

## Mars Hill Church

**Jessop, Harry Briton Leonard.** born 10/15/1887. husband of Maggie Walker. son of Leonard & ?? Jessop.

**Jessop, Maggie M.** born 5/23/1888, died 5/11/1923. wife of Harry Briton Leonard Jessop, daughter of ? Sutton (adopted by ? Walker).

**Jessop, Martha Jean.** age 8d, died 11/16/1942. daughter of Mitchell Jessop (No stone).

**Jessop, Marvelle Marie.** born 1914, died 11/17/1938. wife of Grant Jessop daughter of ? Smith (Johnson Funeral Home Marker).

**Jessop, Mary Mamie.** born 7/11/1905, died 6/25/1933. wife of Jacob W. Jessop. daughter of Calvin & Navy Blocart Hubler.

**Jessop, Mary.** born 1/5/1918, died 1/5/1918.

**Jessop, Richard Wayne.** born 1960, died 1960.

**Jessop, Ronald Leroy.** born 7/20/1949, died 8/2/1949. son of Benjamin M. & Rose Clarkson Jessop (Johnson Funeral Home Marker).

**Jessop, Rosa.** died 3/1/1931.

**Jessop, Wilma M.** born 1/1939, died 2/13/1939. daughter of Jacob & Mary Mamie Hubler Jessop.

Photo by Michael W. Lemberger

**Kees, Joseph.** age 10y 7m, died 7/22/1859. son of D. & S. ? Kees. died on way to Iowa from cholera, buried at Thomas Clark's home. (No stone).

**Laughridge, George W.** born 7/28/1860, died 1924. husband of Sarah A. Garrison.

**Laughridge, Hattie A.** born 2/3/189, died 5/17/1891. daughter of George W. & Sarah A. Garrison Laughridge.

**Laughridge, Sarah Lusette.** born 11/7/1887, died 1/29/1929. daughter of George W. and Saran Ann Garrison Laughridge.

**Laughridge, Sarah A.** born 6/19/1862, died 8/21/1934. wife of George W. Laughridge. daughter of Addison A. Garrison.

**Laverein, Clement.** age 9y, died 11/12/1881. born Chickasaw Co. Iowa.

**Loy, Emily Loy.** born 1855, died 1917. 1st husband was John H. Loy. 3rd husband was James C. Post. daughter of Lewis Z. & Mary M. Smith Rupe.

**Loy, Harold G.** son of Stephen & Minerva Starr Loy.

**Loy, James M.** small stone between cedars row 7.

Mars Hill Church

**Loy, John H.** born 1852, died 1892. 1st wife was Emily Rupe. son of Stephen & Minerva Starr Loy.

**Martin, Andrew.** age 58y 5m 15d, died 7/15/1866. husband of Hilda ?

**Mathews, Harriet L.** age 42y 5m 2d, died 11/16/1867. wife of William Mathews.

**McCauley, Charles Ellis.** age 9y 4m 6d, died 7/9/1877. son of Joseph & Harriet Jane Smith McCauley.

**McCauley, Charles Ellis.** died 3/12/1877. son of John & Martha J. Young McCauley. Charles drowned coming home from school.

**McCauley, Lorena Alverta.** age 1y 11m, died 11/30/1878. daughter of Joseph & Harriet Jane Smith McCauley.

Photo by Michael W. Lemberger

**McCauley, Samuel Merrill.** 1y 10m 17d, died 7/31/1876. son of Joseph & Harriet Jane Smith McCauley.

**McCauley, William Henry.** born 1/16/1857, died 9/21/1871. Killed in cane mill accident.

**McKay, Ralph.** age 74y, died 12/26/1882. born Scotland.

**McLain, Elizabeth Jane.** age 73y, died 2/24/1898. (Davis County Death Book 2).

**Meek, Camino?** age 1m 5d, died 12/18/1859. daughter of John W. & Lucy Ann Monroe Meek (repaired stone).

**Meek, Lucy Ann.** age 23y 2m 6d, died 1/9/1860. wife of John Meek. daughter of ? Monroe.

**Monroe, Daniel H.** age 18y 7m 1d, died 2/6/1862. son of Sanders & Catherine Hougland Monroe, born in Indiana, 1st Civil War soldier to be buried Mars Hill. "He took the measels (sic) at Keokuk, was sent home to die, the measels (sic) settled on his brain." CO D 15th IA Infantry, Civil War.

**Monroe, Ester Cordie.** born 9/9/1854, died 1/14/1875. daughter of Wesley Soul & Margaret Monroe (stolen stone).

**Monroe, Eva S.** born 10/22/1863, died 12/28/1870. daughter of Wesley Soul & Margaret Monroe.

**Monroe, Ida L.** born 9/6/1865, died 1/3/1871. daughter of Wesley Soul & Margaret Monroe.

Photo by Michael W. Lemberger

**Monroe, John W.** age 5y 10m 10d, died 5/24/1859. son of Sanders A. Monroe & Catherine Hougland (stolen stone).

**Monroe, Phebe Parham.** age 87y 3m 19d, died 8/21/1881. wife of Wm. Monroe born WV.

**Monroe, William.** age 74y 4m 2d, died 3/24/1863. husband of Phoebe Parham. son of William and Margaret Whitesides Monroe.

**Niles, Francis E.** born 5/1/1862, died 1/20/1909.

**Owsley, Infant.** died 3/11/1863. son of Matthew & Sara Ann ? Owsley.

**Owsley, Sara Ann.** age 28y 7m 11d, died 7/24/1866. wife of Matthew A. Owsley.

**Owsley, William H.** age 10m 16d, died 6/3/1865. son of Matthew A. & Sara Ann ? Owsley.

**Parker, Elizabeth M.** born 2/15/1871, died 6/15/1953. wife of James M. Parker.

## Mars Hill Church

**Parker, Harry W.** born 5/7/1902, died 11/5/1918. son of James M. & Elizabeth M. ? Parker.

**Parker, James M.** born 1875, died 1961. husband of Elizabeth M. ?

**Patterson, Mary A.** age 78y 11m 24d, died 5/21/1881. wife of John Patterson.

**Pherigo, Stella Mae.** born 12/3/1896, died 6/10/1952. 1st wife of Wendell Pherigo, daughter of Aaron & Alice Snell Post (Johnson Funeral Home Marker).

**Pherigo, Wendell E.** born 1/20/1894, died 2/17/1967. husband of Stella Post. son of John & Angeline Moughler Pherigo. PFC 63rd Field Artillery, WW I.

**Pilcher, Carl C.** born 5/5/1907, died 10/28/1908. son of Homer Elmer & C. M. ? Pilcher.

**Pilcher, Charles A.** born 12/7/1884, died 7/2/1885. son of Thomas J. & Elizabeth Ryan Pilcher.

**Pilcher, Elizabeth.** born 11/21/1847, died 3/19/1921. wife of Thomas J. Pilcher. daughter of Joseph & Hannah Rhine Ryan.

**Pilcher, Frank B.** born 12/23/1891, died 7/21/1913. son of John W. & Vinnie Huffman Pilcher.

**Pilcher, Havill Beardsley.** age 68y, died 6/24/1882. wife Mary Ryan. son of Henry & Honor Rude Pilcher.

**Pilcher, Hugh B.** born 1882, died 1942. 2nd husband of Anna Elizabeth Dial. son of Thomas & Elizabeth Ryan Pilcher.

**Pilcher, Hugh.** age 6m, died 9/8/1897. (Davis County Death Book 2).

**Pilcher, Jessie.** born 5/10/1890, died 11/9/1908.

**Pilcher, John W.** age 60y 3m 11d, died 11/8/1892?? 1st wife was Vinnie Huffman (1/17/1889) 2nd wife was Martha Ellen Meyers (1/21/1900). son of Havilla B. & Mary Ryan Pilcher.

**Pilcher, Mary.** age 73y 3m 18d, died 2/3/1917.

**Pilcher, Thomas J.** born 3/3/1848, died 1/4/1903. husband of Elizabeth Ryan. son of Henry & Honor Rude Pilcher. CO C 47th IA Infantry, Civil War.

**Pilcher, Vinnie.** born 2/5/1871, died 3/9/1898. wife of John Pilcher. daughter of Andrew & Catherine Shank Huffman.

**Porter, George C.** died 8/26/1897. (Davis County Death Book 2).

# A Living Legacy

## Mars Hill Church

**Post, Aaron Milroy.** born 4/15/1862, died 5/16/1928. 1st wife was Alice Snell. 2nd wife was Florence Mable Laughridge. son of Abraham Rosebone & Mary Ione Banford Post (Wagler Funeral Home Marker).

**Post, Abigail.** born 4/11/1886, died 10/12/1940. wife of Edward Post (cousins), daughter of Abraham R. & Isabel Aulger Post.

**Post, Arthur Milroy.** born 5/30/1908, died 10/14/1987. husband of Bessie McMath. son of Aaron & Florence Laughridge Post (Johnson Funeral Home Marker).

**Post, Charles Edward.** born 12/28/1918, died 1974. husband of Louise Murphy (Johnson Funeral Home Marker).

**Post, Edward.** born 4/19/1880, died 11/23/1962. husband of Abigail Post (cousins), son of William & Delilah Crandell Post.

**Post, Florence Mabel.** born 6/1/1883, died 1944. second wife of Aaron M. Post. daughter of George W. & Sarah L. Laughridge (Wagler Funeral Home Marker).

**Post, George D. Sr.** born 3/28/1917, died 7/8/1988. husband of Marjorie May Snelling. son of Aaron M. & Florence Laughridge Post.

**Post, Glen W.** born 6/26/1903, died 6/15/1959. son of Edward & Abigail ? Post.

**Post, Hubert Dean.** born 1942, died 1942. (Wagler Funeral Home Marker).

**Post, Isabell.** born 1/2/1837, died 6/29/1910. wife of Abraham Rosebone Post, daughter of John & Mary Aulger Post.

**Post, John Austin.** born 3/24/1873, died 9/15/1954. son of Abraham R. & Isabel Aulger Post.

**Post, Louise G.** born 2/12/1917, died 8/12/1987. 1st husband was A. Gordon, second husband was Charles Post. daughter of Joseph & Bessie Blangett Murphy (Johnson Funeral Home Marker).

**Post, Marjorie May.** born 12/18/1922, died 8/9/1990. wife of George D. Post, daughter of Benjamin & Daisy A. Kirk Snelling.

**Post, Emily.** born 1855, died 3/27/1917. wife of James Post. daughter of Lewis Zirkle and Mary M. Smith Rupe.

**Post, Robert Dean.** born 10/5/1941, died 12/3/1941. son of George D. & Marjorie M. Snelling Post.

**Post, Stella.** born 9/15/1870. daughter of Wm. Wycoff & Delilah Crandall Post.

A Living Legacy

Photo by Michael W. Lemberger

**Post, Steven.** born 12/5/1905, died 12/18/1905. infant son of James Madison & Myrtle Rhoades Post.

**Post, Steven Marion.** died 8/14/1926. infant son of James Madison and Myrtle Rhoades Post.

**Post, William Wycoff.** age 79y 3m 15d, died 5/3/1918. born 1/18/1839 in PA, died in Belnap, IA. 1st wife was Delilah Crandall, 2nd wife was "Fanny" Elizabeth Francis Sebern Foster. CO F 103rd IL, Civil War.

**Poston, Raymond.** died 11/5/1890. (Davis County Death Book 1 page 74) (No stone).

**Rambo, Elizabeth.** age 73y 6m 7d, died 3/9/1873. wife of Joel Rambo.

**Rambo, Joel M.** age 83y, died 2/26/1872. husband of Elizabeth Ryan.

**Ramsey, Ina L.** born 1919, died 1999. (Reece Funeral Home Marker).

**Reschke, Anna L.** age 59y 10m 17d, died 9/8/1878. wife of M. Reschke.

**Roberts, Charles F.** born 1920, died 1968. husband of Ella June Snelling Roberts.

**Roberts, Ella June.** born 6/20/1924, died 12/11/2003. wife of Charles F. Roberts. daughter of Benjamin & Daisy A. Kirk Snelling.

**Rullman, Bernice.** age 5y 26d, died 1/2/1893. daughter of G. W. & M. E.? Rullman.

## Mars Hill Church

**Rullman, Eva May.** age 3y 10m 6d, died 6/25/1895. daughter of G. W. & M. E.? Rullman.

**Rupe, Addison.** born 1853, died 9/29/1935. (Father).

**Rupe, Almyra Marty.** born 10/27/1859, died 3/28/1922. wife of Lewis Zirkle Rupe, daughter of Henry Harrison & Lydia Ward McNair.

**Rupe, Anna May.** born 5/23/1868, died 10/11/1960. wife of Wayne Rupe, daughter of ? Turner.

**Rupe, Claude Leslie.** born 12/19/1907. died 2/7/1911. son of Fred & Hettie Streeby Rupe (died from spinal meningitis).

**Rupe, Daniel.** age 16y 5m 21d, died 3/21/1879. son of Lewis Z. & Mary M. Smith Rupe.

**Rupe, Dora Morris.** born 2/24/1905, died 12/29/1983. husband of Elvy "Pete". daughter of Charles & Emma Agee Morris.

**Rupe, Elvy "Pete".** born 9/20/1898, died 10/27/1962. husband of Dora Morris. daughter of Thayer & Belle Bailey Rupe.

**Rupe, Guy.** born 7/8/1872, died 6/3/1895. son of John M. & Mary Jane Gee Rupe.

**Rupe, Jim Alan.** born 6/9/1952, died 2/17/1984. husband of Nora Baldridge. son of Alfred & Maxine Blomgreen Rupe.

Photo by Michael W. Lemberger

## A Living Legacy

**Rupe, John Martin.** husband of Mary Jane Gee. son of Lewis Zirkle & Mary M. Smith Rupe. CO E 36th IA Infantry, Civil War.

**Rupe, Lee.** born 12/7/1928, died 6/29/2006. husband of Betty Rae Huddelston (buried elsewhere), son of Elvy "Pete" & Dora Myrtle "Dode" Morris Rupe.

**Rupe, Lewis.** age 10y 11m 3d, died 9/29/1886. son of John M. & Mary J. Gee Rupe.

**Rupe, Lewis Zirkle.** age 72y 1m 20d, died 3/24/1896. husband of Mary Magdalene Smith, son of John Henry & Rebecca Lewis Rupe.

**Rupe, Mary Jane.** born 10/1/1846, died 8/13/1905. wife of John Martin. daughter of Solomon & Hannah Donaldson Gee.

**Rupe, Mary Magdalene.** age 72y 8m 6d, died 5/22/1898. wife of Lewis Zirkle Rupe. daughter of Solomon & Catherine Hartsook Smith.

**Rupe, Nellie.** age 1m, died 3/15/1902. daughter of Addison Rupe & Almyra ? (No stone).

**Rupe, Nora S.** born 1953.

**Rupe, Orin Patrick.** born 9/11/1898, died 2/25/1989. 1st wife was Ada Stamper, 2nd wife was Helen ?. son of Wayne & Anna Turner Rupe.

**Rupe, Wayne.** born 11/16/1868, died 11/10/1914. husband of Anna May Turner. son of John Martin & Mary Jane Gee Rupe.

**Ryan, Howard Joseph.** CO D 15th IA Infantry, Civil War (No stone). Scrapbook belonging to Minnie Hancock.

**Ryan, Sis Ann.** age 27y, died 1/22/1882. wife of John Ryan. daughter of Alexander & Anna ? Weddle.

**Sedore, Cynthia.** age 6y 9d, died 10/10/1898. daughter of Jacob Sedore & Rachel E. Bailey.

**Sedore, Mary E.** age 12y 23d, died 2/21/1877. daughter of Harry & Eliza Jane Long Sedore.

**Shank, Garry Max.** age 6 days, died 8/26/1941. son of Harry Max & Ora Darlene Halfhill Shank.

**Shank, Harry.** born 9/15/1886, died 7/22/1971. husband of Orpha ? son of "Coon" & ? ? Shank.

**Shank, John Robert.** died 2/16/1924. (no stone).

# Mars Hill Church

**Shank, W. T.** (no information)

**Smith, Anthony.** age 67y 4m 20d, died 10/28/1870.

**Smith, Caroline R.** age 36y, died 2/14/1881. born Ohio (no stone).

**Smith, Jacob.** age 24y 7m 17d, died 1862. son of Anthony & Mary A. Smith.

**Smith, Lewis.** age 27y 10m 12d, died 1864. son of Anthony & Mary A. Smith. died during the war at 27 years. CO I 1st IA Cavalry, Civil War.

**Smith, Martha.** daughter of Anthony & M. A. ? Smith.

**Smock, Abraham.** born 7/28/1818, died 6/3/1863. husband of Sarah Catherine Monroe. son of Archibald Cameron & Hannah Moore Smock. CO C 7th IA Cavalry, Civil War.

**Smock, Charles.** age 45y 11m 3d, died 5/15/1889. husband of Sarah Catherine Smock (cousins). son of Archibald & Hannah Moore Smock. CO D 15th IA Infantry, Civil War.

**Smock, Della L.** age 11m 25d, died 7/22/1870. daughter of Felix Thomas & Belle Donaldson Smock.

Photo by Michael W. Lemberger

Photo by Michael W. Lemberger

**Smock, Felix Thomas.** age 24y, died 3/31/1870. husband of Isabelle Davidson. son of Abraham & Sarah Catherine Monroe Smock. born 8/13/1845 in Indiana. CO C 7th IA Cavalry, Civil War.

**Smock, Rachel.** age 88y 4m 9d, died 10/28/1861. wife of Samuel Smock. daughter of Geradus & Rachel Demarest Ryker.

**Smock, William Jerrod.** born 1/26/1840, died 7/14/1864. son of Abraham Smock & Sarah Catherine Monroe. born 2/4/1840 in Indiana. CO I 1st Iowa Cavalry, Civil War, Killed Little Rock, AK. Buried in National Cemetery, Little Rock grave # 723, Memorial stone only at Mars Hill.

**Snelling, Benjamin Cleveland.** born 2/9/1888, died 10/2/1951. (Reece Funeral Home marker.)

**Snelling, Daisy Agnes.** born 5/29/1887, died 5/11/1970. (Reece Funeral Home marker.)

**Snelling, George W.** born 1909, died 1972. WWII (Reece Funeral Home Marker).

**Snyder, Linda Joan.** born 5/5/1945, died 10/6/2006. wife of Robert Ray Snyder. daughter of Virgil O. & Ellen Jessop Williams.

**Stadter, Edward.** age 3y 7m 1d, died 4/25/1865. son of F. W. & M. L. ? Stadter.

**Stadter, Emily.** age 6m, died 4/15/1865. daughter of F. W. & M. L. ? Stadter.

**Stadter, Henry.** age 15y 11m 3d, died 2/7/1875. son of F. W. & M. L. ? Stadter.

## Mars Hill Church

**Stadter, John W.** age 17y, died 8/22/1864. son of F. W. & M. L. ? Stadter.

**Talley, Infant.** born 1898, died 1898. daughter of Thomas & Eva ? Talley.

**Talley, Irene.** born 11/28/1895, died 12/31/1895. daughter of Thomas & Eva ? Talley.

**Taylor, James.** born 6/28/1820, died 12/11/1895. husband of Starling ?

**Taylor, Starling.** born 8/14/1846, died 6/20/1901. wife of James Taylor.

**Thomas, Benjamin Thomas.** age 94y 11m 22d, died 5/12/1902, 1st wife was Patience Thompson, 2nd wife was Mary (Eggers) Willis. son of John & Catherine Putman Thomas.

**Thomas, Effie M.** age 1y 5m 22d, died 9/2/1888. daughter of Elijah W. & Sara A. Sedore Thomas.

**Thomas, George E.** age 25y 3m 4d, died 11/12/1892. husband of Alice Small. son of Benjamin & Mary Eggers Willis Thomas.

**Thomas, Harvey.** born 3/4/1897, died 1/25/1898. son of Elijah & Sara Sedore Thomas.

**Thomas, Ira E.** died 1/13/1904 ?? son of Matthew & Roseana Rupe Thomas.

**Thomas, Irrie Urvie.** born 1/13/1903, died 2/15/1903. son of Grant & Amy Sedore Thomas.

**Thomas, Mary.** age 86y, died 3/12/1912. 1st husband was Wream Willis, 2nd husband was Benjamin Thomas. daughter of Benam & Lida Dollars Eggers.

**Thomas, Rae.** born 1904. (Campbell Funeral Home Marker).

**Thomas, Willie.** born 12/10/1917, died 3/20/1918. son of Grant & Amy Sedore Thomas.

**Turner, Edwin Ray.** age 17y 8m 2d, died 5/18/1898. son of William Frank & Mary Rupe Turner.

**Turner, Infant.** born 12/22/1911, died 12/22/1911. infant of Ross & Katherine Coughlin Turner.

**Waller, George Curtis.** born 2/22/1900, died 6/9/1963. son of Joe & Doris Garrelson Waller.

**Watson, Clara.** born 10/?/1888, died 8/20/1889. daughter of William & Elzina ? Watson (No stone.)

## A Living Legacy

**Watson, Infant.** born 6/23/1894, died 6/23/1894. unknown male (No stone.)

**Watts, Catherine.** born 9/25/1816, died 9/4/1897. wife of John B. Watts.

**Watts, Eva or Iva? Ellen.** age 1y 6m 13d, died 1897. parents unknown.

**Wayland, Walter.** born 1870, died 1933. husband of Sylvia Donaldson.

**Wayne, Richard.** born 1960, died 1960. parents unknown (No stone.)

**Weddle, Alexander.** born 4/26/1810, died 9/1/1872. husband of Anna ?

**Weddle, Anna.** born 3/26/1811, died 5/14/1888. wife of Alexander Weddle.

**Wheatley, David Leroy.** born 10/20/1946, died 10/21/1946. son of Carl W. & Margaret Porter Wheatly (No stone.)

**Williams, Ellen Belle.** born 4/9/1920, died 10/23/1995. wife of Virgil O. Williams. daughter of Leonard & Maggie Sutton Jessop.

**Williams, Virgil O.** born 6/14/1914, died 7/27/1987. husband of Ellen Jessop. son of Owen & Ethel Williams Jessop. Pvt. US Army, WW II.

Photo by Michael W. Lemberger

**Willis, John E.** age 34y 5m 12d, died 9/9/1878. son of Wrean S. & Mary Eggers Willis Thomas. CO B 137th IL Infantry (100 day 1864), Civil War.

**Wolfe, Carolyn M.** born 1/6/1942, died 8/29/2005. wife of Donald Wolfe, daughter of Richard & Beatrice Carver Miller.

**Wood, Maggie.** age 3 days, died 9/23/1898. Wapello County Death Book 2 Page 150.

**Yoder, Daniel.** age 62y, died 1/4/1911. (No stone.)

> **RuN!!!**
>
> Oct 5, 1972
>
> Sherry Campbell, Cindy Bodkine, Donna Simmons, + Juansetta Clark was here Thursday morning, skipping school. We are going to inform you of our mishap. We all were walking through the cemetary and one of the old tombstones started to move and the grave cracked open. We soon left! This happened a week ago and we came back to write it down in Satan's book! Leave before something happens to YOU!

## VANDALISM & THE OCCULT

The isolated location of the church and the cemetery surrounding it have prompted vandalism and led to persistent rumors that Mars Hill is haunted.

Over the years, stories have circulated of mysterious lights appearing in the cemetery, of figures wearing Civil War uniforms riding cavalry horses on the road past the church, of mysterious wails and moans resounding from a nearby trestle bridge where a young woman is supposed to have tossed her newly-baptized infant to its death at some vague time in the past.

But the stories fade away when investigated. They seem always to have happened to "someone", at some undefined time. No evidence -- such as names, dates, or specifics -- seems to ever be available to support the allegations of ghostly sightings.

One unpleasant tale concerning Mars Hill Church is true, however. In the late 1970s, occult groups surfaced in south central Iowa, and Mars Hill Church became a focal point for Satanic activities. In June of 1985, caretaker Reva Rupe found a

# A Living Legacy

Photo by Michael W. Lemberger

## Mars Hill Church

**Vandalism discouraging to Mars Hill trustees**

mutilated black cat hanging over the church altar. Satanic crosses and symbols had been painted in blood on the walls. Historic tombstones were broken off. Pews were stacked and set on fire inside the church. Later, vandals dragged the remaining pews out into the lawn in front of the church, stacked them and set them on fire.

Fortunately the church itself didn't burn as a result of these incidents, but the worst was yet to come.

---

My husband and I entered the church and looked up in shock and amazement at what we saw. The vandals had been working very hard. They had ripped all of the old straight-backed pews apart and stacked them near the front of the church in the shape of a teepee. Someone had climbed the teepee to the ceiling gand chopped a hole in it. The vandals had made a pile of kindling near the base of the teepee and tried to make a fire, but it didn't burn and the church was still with us.

Members of the board cleaned up the mess and we were ready for the annual meeting. One of the speakers that year had a wonderful message about Mars Hill sitting on Holy Ground because the pioneers had dedicated it to God when it was built and it was still here. My husband told her after the service that her message was so appropriate because someone had recently tried to burn the church down... It was a turning point for me. I decided that day that I would do whatever I could to preserve this little bit of history, and I cannot hear the song "Holy Ground" without getting the shivers.

-- *Donna Smithhart*

## A Living Legacy

Stones are braced to hold them in place while repairs harden.

Members of the State Association for the Preservation of Iowa Cemeteries (SAPIC) met at Mars Hill Cemetery in 2006 to work on restoring gravestones.

# Mars Hill Church

One fine day a few years ago, I was pleasantly surprised when the three pretty fifth-grade girls who lived in our block stopped by to visit. I invited them in and their eyes immediately fell on our collection of Mars Hill art work on the living room wall. One of them blurted out, "That's Mars Hill, the church that is haunted and has all the ghosts."

I told them I went out there quite often and I had never seen a single ghost. I asked them if they would like to go to Mars Hill and see for themselves... Shortly after there was a beautiful warm fall day and we went on our field trip. Our great-grandson Tynan went along for the ride.

When we arrived at the church, we discovered that the Japanese beetles had got there first. The church, trees, every headstone -- and soon all of us -- were covered with them. But we were there on a mission and so we went about the business of exploring Mars Hill.

I told them of the pioneers who had settled this area so many years ago and how they had felt the need to have a place to worship together. They had built this log cabin church one log at a time, after dragging the logs in out of the surrounding forest. I told them the church was still used a few times a year for church services and an occasional wedding. I told them about all the tourists who come here to enjoy this special place. Then I asked them how they knew of Mars Hill's spooky reputation. They said everyone knew that. I think that is true, but it is good for kids to hear the real story and maybe they will pass that on, too.

We visited the cemetery and everyone picked out their favorite headstone and had their picture taken beside it. We brushed the bugs off each other and went back to town.

-- *Donna Smithhart*

**Tynan Smithhart with his favorite headstone**

A Living Legacy

# THE FIRE

On Thursday, March 9, 2006, Mars Hill Church was severely damaged by fire. Firefighters were called to the church at about 8 a.m. after a woman who lived nearby saw smoke and flames. The first firefighters to respond were from nearby Floris. They found the interior ablaze and the roof already gone. By the time the Wapello County Rural Fire Department reached the scene, the flames had been knocked down and only heavy smoke remained.

Though portions of all four walls still stood after the fire, two walls were severely damaged, the roof was gone, and the plank floor was charred and crumbling.

# Mars Hill Church

# A Living Legacy

Within days, five Wapello County teenagers – ages 15 to 19 – were charged in connection with the arson, which is defined in Iowa law as either the intentional burning of a structure or setting a fire that would reasonably be expected to result in a structure fire.

# Mars Hill Church

## A Living Legacy

One teen pleaded no contest; the others pleaded guilty to varying charges. The court ordered restitution to be made.

A local historian speculated that the arsonists may have been convinced that the church was possessed and believed that it would not burn.

Aftermath of the fire.

A Living Legacy

"A church is made up of the people. The physical structure is simply a building. And that will be restored."   – *Don Bramschreiber, board president*

## Mars Hill Church

Bracing was installed to stabilize the walls.

# A Living Legacy

Inside west wall looking out, after the fire

# Mars Hill Church

Back wall of church, showing chimney where it fell after the fire

# A Living Legacy

Inside the east wall, after the fire

## Mars Hill Church

Though the church was not usable in the summer of 2006,
the annual reunion went on as scheduled on the grounds.

Benjamine Post's drawing reflects on the church and the loss,
as well as the music during the celebration.

# REBUILDING

Immediately after the fire, the structure was stabilized and braced to keep the remains from collapsing. Efforts began to preserve what remained and rebuild if possible.

At first, there were doubts that Mars Hill could be saved. The damage appeared too severe and the estimated costs of rebuilding seemed too high. Initial estimates for rebuilding the church were more than $114,000, a vast sum for a congregation and board of trustees which were accustomed to relying on a free-will offering at its annual meeting to supply operating funds.

Further inspection indicated that many of the logs were only superficially charred and could be salvaged. Still, the workers faced an enormous challenge. An application for grant funding, filed in early 2007, puts the problem into perspective: "To begin

The site after the remaining log walls were disassembled for restoration.

restoration, the building will have to be disassembled one log at a time by hand. Those logs will have to be labeled as to their location in the original structure. Then those logs will need to be cleaned, and the cement chinking removed. The floor cannot be saved and the foundation needs repaired."

Similar materials from another building of the period, a local two-story log cabin made of hand-hewn logs, were donated to the cause. When the damaged floor was removed, more logs were found underneath, forming the original foundation, and some of them were recycled to replace logs damaged by the fire. Period lumber from a local barn was donated to form the new flooring, and a wooden ceiling was obtained from a nearly house which dated from the period.

Local contractors pitched in, and board members and church supporters volunteered time and materials to clear the site, dismantle and number the damaged logs, haul away debris, plane off charred wood, and start to rebuild.

Terrasol Restoration and Renovation of St. Peter, Minnesota, was hired to create a restoration plan. Contractor Glen O'Dell and Mars Hill board member Benjamine Post

# A Living Legacy

Hauling away the fire debris.

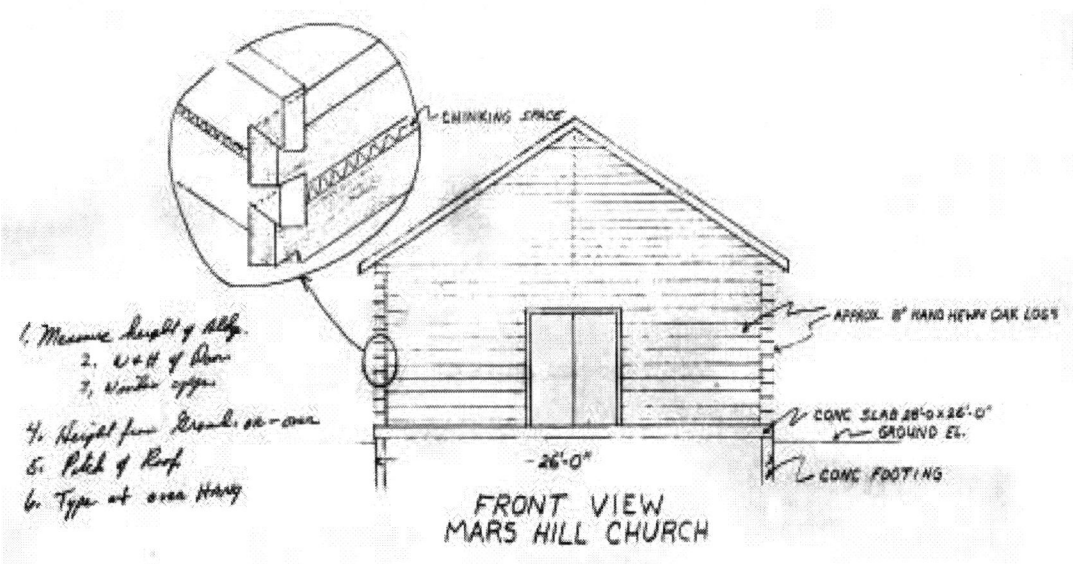

FRONT VIEW
MARS HILL CHURCH

# Mars Hill Church

The new foundation slab.

Preparing the logs.

## A Living Legacy

went to Terrasol's headquarters in Minnesota for training on how to salvage the logs and how to assemble a log building. Workers used bicarbonate of of soda to clean the logs and "draw knives" to plane the burned portions from the logs. It was necessary to pare each salvaged log down to a clean wood surface so the mortar chinking would stick between the logs.

# Mars Hill Church

# A Living Legacy

Fifteen months after the fire, the site had been cleared. New footings and the concrete foundation slab were poured, and reconstruction began, again with volunteers assisting in each step of the work.

Companies hired to work on the reconstruction offered discounts; a local company loaned a crane truck to lift the 28-foot-long logs; an area farmer used his end loader to clear debris, and a locally owned trucking service hauled load after load of debris and refused payment.

# A Living Legacy

143

## Mars Hill Church

# A Living Legacy

# Mars Hill Church

# A Living Legacy

# Mars Hill Church

Photo by Michael W. Lemberger

A Living Legacy

1-24-07

# Supervisors put support behind Mars Hill Church restoration efforts

**BY MATT MILNER**
COURIER STAFF WRITER

OTTUMWA — Efforts to restore Mars Hill Church already had widespread backing from southeast Iowans. Now they can add financial support from the Wapello County Board of Supervisors.

Church board member Jody Bresch told the supervisors Tuesday that the community supports rebuilding, but that they need help from elected officials as well. She asked for a letter of support from the board and a financial contribution. The letter was never in doubt. Finances are tight, though.

"How much are you looking at asking for?" asked Supervisor Mike Petersen.

Bresch never put a specific figure forward for the request. Supervisor Steve Siegel proposed $5,000 for now. The door remains open for future contributions, but much depends on the budget process and where other needs are in Wapello County.

"There's a lot of demands for the money," Siegel said.

The church burned in March 2006 after authorities say several teenagers built a fire inside. Two still await trial. Bresch said full restitution has been ordered for the others and one has begun payments. But the longer the church board waits, the more expensive rebuilding will be. That means things must happen sooner rather than later and makes it difficult to wait for restitution.

"The odds of seeing any of that money any time in the near term is not good," she said.

Donations are coming in. Many of the major donors are area churches and the Ottumwa High School Student Council donated a quarter of the proceeds from a school dance. Bresch said the board has just about $44,000 on hand. That includes cash and physical assets. The cost of restoring the church was initially estimated at more than $100,000.

"This is primarily a salvage and restoration project. We have enough of the original materials left to be worth our restoration efforts," Bresch said. "To begin restoration the structure will have to be disassembled, one log at a time by hand."

The physical assets include logs from the church and other rebuilding materials. Those are key. Hand-hewn logs are not common, but many logs from the church itself are salvageable. Others have turned up and are accessible to the church rebuilding efforts.

Supervisors wanted to make sure the church is less vulnerable to future problems. Bresch said the church board plans to install a security system with links to the Wapello County Sheriff's Department. Siegel also pressed Bresch on access to the church.

"I know before the building was always open. Is that going to change?" he asked

"I think the way we're headed is it's going to be open by appointment," Bresch responded.

*Matt Milner can be reached at (641) 683-5359 or via e-mail at mwmilner@mchsi.com*

Fund-raising efforts included a benefit auction, concerts, raffles, and donations from churches, businesses and individuals. The Ottumwa High School student council donated part of the proceeds of a school dance.

Artist P. Buckley Moss donated a remarqued, signed and numbered print of her limited edition print, "Mars Hill Remembered." The print was auctioned on eBay to raise funds for the rebuilding effort.

## A Living Legacy

Above: Brian Hoffman at Christ Church

Right: Ottumwa Courier editorial

**OUR OPINION**

# Mars Hill: Preserving history

We lost part of our heritage when fire destroyed much of the historic Mars Hill Church. Now, thanks to some southern Iowans who want to keep that heritage alive, the popular country church building is lovingly being rebuilt.

Many of the old logs used to frame the building were damaged in the arson fire in March 2006.

Since then, a group of church lovers and volunteers have been working to see that the church would rise again.

The site is on a hill top south of Ottumwa near the Wapello/Davis county line. You have to know where you're going to find the church which hadn't been used much in recent years.

A group would gather annually for a picnic and church services.

And, the building had seen its share of vandalism due to its out-of-the-way location.

As workers hew logs and plan frames, the church is slowly going up. They've tried to save as many of the old logs as possible which has required a lot of time and effort to clean them up. Historical accuracy is a major goal, but some adaptations were necessary such as putting a cement base under the authentic wood floor.

With the new building will come added security in hopes that such a tragedy doesn't happen again.

The church was constructed in 1856 by Iowa pioneers who dragged hand-hewn logs to the top of Mars Hill. They wanted a place to worship and found an ideal spot.

Somehow, it lasted throughout the years and into another century. It was placed on the National Register of Historic Places in 1974.

Not enough can be said for the drive and dedication of all those who are giving of their time to see that the church is located on Mars Hill once again.

The generosity of many is commendable. Time has been donated, money has been given along with materials and effort. Local companies have provided huge discounts, free labor and loans of equipment.

Thank you for giving the church back to our corner of the state. We need to preserve our heritage.

# BENEFIT AUCTION FOR MARS HILL LOG CHURCH

FOR THE RESTORATION OF THE CHURCH

**SATURDAY, OCTOBER 21, 2006 - 10:00 A.M.**

SALE TO BE CONDUCTED AT

**FAMILY LIFE CENTER, ASSEMBLY OF GOD, 103 KD AVE., ELDON, IOWA 52554**

**ANTIQUES AND COLLECTABLES:** Very unique organ stool w/turned legs and braces, horizontal grooves on center post and legs, metal claw feet with glass balls, adjustable seat, stool has a back rest, two outside spindles, turned 5 center spindles, straight carvings on top of back; 32 barbie dolls, 28 in original boxes; cast iron skillets; #8 Wagner; #3 Wagner; #6 Griswold; #8 Griswold; #8 skillet lid; cast iron tub; flat iron; cast iron dog and irons for fireplace (cast at the Albert Bowers Foundry, Ottumwa, IA); two antique sewing baskets; old postcards; IVA - Lure decorative plate; crocheted and embroidered pieces; hand decorated china tea pot; old newspapers; 1930 Eldon class book; football picture; Eldonian newpaper, and other Eldon memorabilia; class play performed at the opera house; double-faced Jack Sprat ad 10½ by 15½ inches, 1940's from Harmon Brothers Grocery in Eldon, IA, back side of ad features Corn Custard Southern Style recipe incorporated with black art; 8 handmade quilts by local crafters; Susie Weir has donated her last quilt - quilted by "In Stitches Quilt Club" Eldon, IA; 2 handmade baby quilts; 2 handmade wall hangings; hand pieced and machine quilted quilt from Threads of Friendship Quilt Guild of Bloomfield, IA; baseball cards; political button display; pump organ in good working condition; old stamps; large old teddy bear with rubber nose; old wooden egg crate; 2 mallard decoys; Jewel Tea autumn leaf casserole; Currier & Ives chop plate; pie plate; two 9 inch vegetable bowls; ash tray; gravy boat; creamer; old blow torch; wooden box; Amish dolls; limited edition art prints & original artwork by Todd Smithhart.

**REEL TO REEL TAPES OF OLD RADIO PROGRAMS OF THE 40's-50's:** 326 tapes, each tape is 4-6 hours long: Lux Radio Theater, Amos & Andy, Red Skelton, Suspense, Life of Riley, Great Gildersleeve, Cavacade of America, Lone Ranger, The Shadow, Fibber McGee & Molly, Jack Benny, Dragnet, Gunsmoke, CBS News Coverage D Day, Whistler, X Minus One, Six Shooter, 90 different programs. For a complete list, contact us at 641-652-7834 or lzemcrow@yahoo.com and we will email you the list. We will accept telephone or email bids prior to the auction.

**HOUSEHOLD ITEMS & FURNITURE:** New and used table lamps; two upholstered bar stools; coat racks; 3 portable TV's; 2 wooden rocker chairs; wall hangings; 2 loveseats; pine buffet table; small roll top desk; glass top table approx. 42 inches in diameter; 2 recliners; large glass top coffee table; Whirlpool electric stove, very clean; dishes; pots and pans and kitchen utensils.

**HAND CRAFTED ITEMS:** Large hand forged bakers rack with oak shelves; hand forged pot rack; hand forged fireplace set; hand forged quilt rack; cedar patio table with hand forged legs; 2 decorative rolling pins; hand forged double rolling pin holder; handmade wooden chest with cedar lining.

**TOOLS:** New Smith Oxy-acetylene cutting & welding outfit.

**MARS HILL ART:** Matted and framed watercolor print "Decoration Day Mars Hill" #11/450 by Melody Coulter, Ottumwa, IA; matted and framed Mars Hill photo by Michael W. Lemberger, Ottumwa, IA; very old postcard featuring Mars Hill Church, matted and framed; "Mars Hill 1974 Revisited" pen and ink print by Jeanne Dixon, Bloomfield, IA, matted and framed; pillow depicting Mars Hill Log Church by Kathy McCall, Floris, IA; Ottumwa Courier dated July 1, 1976, photo by Mike Lemberg and article by Loree Roach, both with the Ottumwa Courier, framed and matted by James Weeks.

**ANTIQUE GUNS:** Connecticut Valley Arms black powder 50 cal., octagon barrel; very old 22 cal. single shot rifle, slide action, octagon barrel. This rifle is a Colts P.T.F.A. Mfg. Co., Hartford, Conn. USA Patent May 29, 1883; May 26, '85; June 15, '86; Feb. 26, '87.

**GUNS:** New Knight black powder rifle revolution 50 cal., S.S. barrel.

**MISC.:** Schwin ladies bike; large electric treadmill; Gravity Rider exerciser; like new 18 inch Sears electric lawn mower; Christmas decorations; stuffed animals; 2 new 13" car tires; new and used luggage; like new large Dana Glo kerosene heater; Kimbal Swinger 100 electric organ with bench and music; cookbooks; large selection of what-nots.

**HORSES:** 2 registered quarter horses: Ad Cashin King Black stallion foaled April 23, 2004, sire Hot Shot Dash, dam Binita Glo, sire's parents Dash For Cash top side - Another Hot Idea bottom side, dam's parents Glo Boy King top side - Miss Glo Flight bottom side; bay mare foaled April 23, 2004, sire Flash One, dam TRS Zevis Moon Babe, sire's parents Dash For Perks top side - Flashalli bottom side, dam's parents Iris Zevi top side - Pocos Moon Shadow bottom side.

**PONY:** American show pony weanling can be registered.

**BOER GOAT:** 1 red billy Boer goat kid.

**GIFT CERTIFICATES:** One full page advertisement in the Ottumwa Courier; large selection of gift certificates covering a large range of merchandise and services.

**JEWELRY:** Beautiful necklace featuring the Coal Palace, designed and manufactured by Rhynas of Ottumwa; P. Buckley Moss broach.

**COINS:** 1844 large cent; Indian head pennies, 1891-94, 1907 and others; buffalo nickels 1935-37; three war nickels 1943 P-D-S; silver liberty seated dimes; 1853, 1857, 1891 silver barber dimes; 1907-11-14 silver mercury dimes, 1936 S, 1938 S, 1944 P, 1945 P; silver liberty quarter 1956; silver barber quarter 1899 & 1916 D; silver standing quarters 1925 P, 1926 P; silver Washington quarter 1952; Washington quarter bi-cent; silver walking halves 1934 S, 1941 S; silver Franklin halves 1960-61-62 D; Morgan silver dollars 1979 S, 1880 S, 1881 S, 1883 O, 1896 P, 1896 O, 1901 O, 1921 P, 1921 D, 1921 S; Ike silver dollar 1971 S; Roosevelt dimes 1990 P, 1991 P (UNC); silver piece dollar 1922-23 S 24; two cent 1864; nickel three cent piece 1866 F; several foreign coins; **other coins have been promised. Coins, stamps, and baseball cards will sell at approximately noon.**

**AUCTIONEERS: BILL TROUT, RON SPROUSE, LARRY CROW 641-652-7834**

**TERMS - CASH**

**FOOD AVAILABLE ON THE GROUNDS**

**POSITIVE ID REQUIRED**

ALL ITEMS MUST BE PAID FOR BEFORE REMOVAL. NOT RESPONSIBLE FOR ACCIDENTS. THE INFORMATION WAS OBTAINED FROM OUR MOST RELIABLE SOURCES, HOWEVER, THE AUCTION COMPANY IS NOT RESPONSIBLE FOR ANY ERRORS. ANY ANNOUNCEMENTS DAY OF SALE TAKES PRECEDENCE OVER PRINTED MATERIAL. WE WILL CONTINUE TO EXCEPT GOOD CLEAN MERCHANDISE THRU OCTOBER 19, 2006.

CALL LARRY CROW 641-652-7834 • DON BRAMSCHREIBER 641-684-8113 • TODD SMITHHART 641-684-8608

## A Living Legacy

Photo by Michael W. Lemberger

Edith (Orman) Crist, holding Carol Ann (Crist) Hoffman, 1941. The ceiling of this period house was donated for use in Mars Hill Church.

# Mars Hill Church

**Roof framing is ready to go into place.**

# A Living Legacy

# Mars Hill Church

# A Living Legacy

# Mars Hill Church

# A Living Legacy

Chinking -- filling the spaces between the logs with mortar.

## Mars Hill Church

# A Living Legacy

Painting the gables, soffit, cross -- and name.

# Mars Hill Church

November, 2007.

# A Living Legacy

Photo by Michael W. Lemberger

# Mars Hill Church

Photo by Michael W. Lemberger

The rebuilt church as it appeared in November, 2007.

A Living Legacy

## THE RENEWED CHURCH

About two-thirds of the logs in the original church were salvaged and reused, with replacement logs coming from period buildings nearby. Many came from an old house whose logs matched the dimensions of the church.

The new foundation is a concrete slab with footings set below the frost line. Other modern concessions include an up-to-date security system which is connected to law enforcement agencies.

Split-log benches, thought to be similar to the ones used by the original settlers, will be added to the church.

The wedding of Justin Pfaff and Rachael Estes on October 7, 2007, was the first to be held in the church. Rebuilding was not yet complete.

## Mars Hill Church

Though the walls were up and the roof was on, the logs had not yet been chinked.

# A Living Legacy

Mars Hill Church

# MOVING TO THE FUTURE

An annual meeting is held each summer with a basket dinner at 1:00 P.M. and a business meeting and worship service at 2:00 P.M. The designated date for this annual meeting has changed through the years but is now is the second Sunday in June. The Church is supported by individual contributions and a free will offering at the annual service. The church is also used for funerals, weddings, public meetings, and special ceremonies.

---

### REUNION and ANNUAL MEETING
### JUNE 8, 2008

Rededication of restored church, and dedication of a special gravestone marker for John Donaldson, member of Mars Hill Church and Civil War Medal of Honor Recipient, who is buried in Mars Hill Cemetery.

---

### REUNION AND MEETING INFORMATION FROM 1989-2007

*Special thanks to Donna Smithhart for keeping records for the last eighteen years and making the following information available.*

**MAY 21, 1989** for lunch 53 / meeting 65  Meeting opened by Larry Crow; Singing led by Rev. Clint Spilman; Music by organ– Dan Knight, organist; Special music by Marie Brooks and the Silver Strings; Speaker, Rev. Clint Spilman

**MAY 20, 1990** for lunch 26 / meeting 26  Meeting opened by Larry Crow; Singing led by Gary Grooms; Special Music by Bill & Janice Albert, Eldon; Speaker Rev. John Cooper

**JUNE 9, 1991** for lunch 44 / meeting 44  Meeting opened by Larry Crow; Special Music by Harley Hart and Bill & Janice Albert; Speaker Rev. David Albert, Congregational Church, Eldon

**JUNE 14, 1992** for lunch 45 / meeting 45  Meeting opened by Don Bramschreiber; Singing led by Gary Grooms; Special music by Frank Barnhart and Unga Nicholson; Speaker Don Bramschreiber.

**JUNE 6, 1993** for lunch 33 / meeting 33  Meeting opened by Larry Crow; Singing led by Pastor Roual Nicholson; Special Music by Nicholsons; Speakers Ulga Nicholson and Pastor Roual Nicholson of First Baptist, Ottumwa

**JUNE 11, 1994** for lunch 20 / meeting 34  Meeting opened by Don Bramschreiber; Singing led by Ferve & Jeretta Van Antwerp; Special Music by Ferve & Jeretta Van Antwerp; Speaker Rev. Barry Stewart, Albia Road Baptist, Ottumwa

**JUNE 11, 1995** for lunch 27 / meeting 37  Meeting opened by Don Bramschreiber; Singing led by Gary Grooms; Organist Sheila Grooms; Special Music by Josh Smith & Craig Dooley; Speaker Rev. Rex Wilson, First Baptist, Ottumwa

# A Living Legacy

**JUNE 9, 1996** for lunch 35 / meeting 55  Meeting opened by Don Bramschsreiber; Singing led by Gary Ogren; Special Music by Gary Ogren; Speaker Pastor Bill Payne, Pennsylvania Ave. Church of Christ

**JUNE 8, 1997** for lunch 33 / meeting 38  Meeting opened by Don Bramschreiber; Singing led by Rev. Jesse & Sherrie Elkins; Special Music by Rev. Jesse & Sherrie Elkins; Speaker Rev. Jesse Elkins, Zion Community Church of God

**JUNE 14, 1998** for lunch 21 / meeting 37  Meeting opened by Don Bramschreiber; Singing led by Rev. Rex Wilson; Special Music by Jessica Kurtz; Speaker Rev. David Albert, Living Hope Baptist Church, Eldon

**JUNE 13, 1999** for lunch 12 / meeting 40  Meeting opened by Don Bramschreiber; Singing led by Gary Ogren; Special Music by Gary Ogren; Speaker John Freeman, First Church of the Open Bible, Ottumwa

**JUNE 11, 2000** for lunch 18 / meeting 24  Meeting opened by Don Bramschreiber; Singing led by Gary Ogren; Special Music by Gary Ogren & Sue Yenger; Speaker George Edgerly, First Pentecostal Assembly of God Ottumwa.

**JUNE 10, 2001** for lunch 31 / meeting 31  Meeting opened by Don Bramschreiber; Singing led by Sue Yenger & Marjeane Derby; Special Music by Marjeane Derby and Jessica Kurtz; Speaker Pastor John Cooper, Assembly of God, Eldon.

**JUNE 9, 2002** for lunch 28 / meeting 36  Meeting opened by Don Bramschreiber; Singing led by Marjeane Derby; Special Music by Marjeane Derby; Speaker Rev. Verle Edgerly.

**JUNE 8, 2003** for lunch 21 / meeting 37  Meeting opened by Don Bramschreiber; Singing led by Marjeane Derby; Special Music by Marjeane Derby (solo) Allen Fisher (solo); Speaker Rev. Howard Leasure from Princeton. Special Guest: Helen Davis, a descendant of the Clark family who donated the property in 1850s for site of Mars Hill Church.

**JUNE 13, 2004** for lunch 21 / meeting 21 Meeting Opened by Larry Crow, Chairman; Singing led by MarJeane Derby; Special Music by Ezekiel Elkins, Hannah and Sherrie Elkins; Speaker Rev. Julius Kutzenberg of Belgrade, Missouri.

**JUNE 12, 2005** for lunch 17 / meeting 44  Meeting opened by Don Bramschreiber; Singing led by Henry & Sherry Lippert; Special Music by Sherry Lippert; Speakers Rev. Paul & Lois Frederick, Missionary Alliance Church.

**JUNE 11, 2006** for lunch 27 / meeting 27  Meeting opened by Don Bramschreiber; Singing led by Henry & Sherry Lippert; Special Music by Henry &. Sherry Lippert; Speaker Rev. Henry Lippert, First Baptist Church, Ottumwa.

**JUNE 10, 2007** for lunch 40 / meeting 44  Meeting opened by Don Bramschreiber; Singing led by Eileen Post; Music accompanist Doris Noland; Special Music by Eileen Post accompanying Benjamine Post illustrating the music with chalk drawing; Speaker Father John Spiegel, St. Patrick Church, Ottumwa.

# Mars Hill Church

March 2008.

Photo by Michael W. Lemberger

Photo by Michael W. Lemberger

A Living Legacy

## MARS HILL RIDGE
### By Jody Bresch

The gravel road curved 'round a ridge,
And there, wrapped in antiquity, it stood,
And feeling bewitched, I felt the music
And listened, rapt, to its symphonic history
Where it sang across the years at Mars Hill Woods.

Then I stepped into the musical score
Of one hundred and fifty years gone by
Because it was magic to walk through a door
Where history had walked on hardwood floors
Worn smooth by years of hard-worn lives.

And that mid-noon beside a country track
In a log-cabin church where shutters hung back,
I sniffed the scent of new-mown grass
Sheared short where it wrapped
Around tombstones, bent and cracked.

And later, I told this with a sigh
When all that stood was charcoal shell
Of the dreams these pioneers lived by.
When all seemed lost, a few of us chose to try
To rebuild those dreams in this country vale.

The path we chose took twists and turns
None of us expected. Friendship was one.
Generosity another. Then came family.
By the time the church had been rebuilt
We were sisters and brothers.

*Copyright 2008 Jody Bresch*

> The Mars Hill Board of Trustees wishes to thank all the people and organizations who have supported and assisted in rebuilding Mars Hill Church.

## To Visit Mars Hill Church

**From Ottumwa, Iowa:** Go four miles south on US Highway 63 toward Bloomfield. Turn east onto Copperhead Road. Go four miles to 100th St. and turn right (south) approximately 3 miles to the church.

**From Bloomfield, Iowa:** Go seven miles north on US Highway 63 toward Ottumwa. Turn east on J15 toward Floris. Go three miles to Peach Ave. and turn north for one mile. Bear left onto 125th St. for 0.5 miles. Turn north on Oak Ave. for 0.8 mile. Turn east on Monarch Trail for 0.2 mile. Turn north on Owl Ave. 0.8 miles to the church.

> For more information about Mars Hill:
> Don Bramschreiber   641-684-8113
> Benjamine Post   641-682-6540
> email marshill@netins.net

## About the Authors

**Michael W. Lemberger** is a professional photographer, artist, historian, and teacher. He is the author of *Focus on Photos*, how to take better photographs with any camera; *Pilgrimage: The Mass of Pope John Paul II in Middle America*; *Come Let Us Journey* – the installation of Martin J. Amos as Bishop of Davenport; *Meet Me at the Fair*, a photographic history of the St. Louis World's Fair, and two photographic histories of his hometown of Ottumwa, Iowa – *Ottumwa*, co-authored with Wilson J. Warren, and *Ottumwa in Postcards*.

He was a newspaper photographer for many years, winning more than 100 national, regional, and state awards for excellence in photography. As an artist, he creates intricate pen and ink drawings. His collection of historic photographs has been called the most extensive and best-documented privately-held photo collection in existence.

His website is www.mlemberger.com.

**LeAnn Lemberger** is better-known as Leigh Michaels, the award-winning author of more than 80 contemporary romance novels published in 25 languages and 120 countries, with 30 million copies in print. She is also the author of several non-fiction books including *On Writing Romance*, a main book club selection from Writers Digest Books. She is the co-author of *Ottumwa in Postcards*; *Focus on Photos*, how to take better photographs with any camera, and *Meet Me at the Fair*, a photographic history of the St. Louis World's Fair.

She teaches writing online at Gotham Writers' Workshop (writingclasses.com).

Her website is www.leighmichaels.com.

## Other books from PBL Limited
*Publishing & Book Distribution*

Focus on Photos $24.99
St. Patrick's Georgetown $24.99
Concerning Mary Ann $26.99
Mars Hill: A Living Legacy $24.99
Meet Me At the Fair $19.99
"Come, Let Us Journey" $19.99
Pilgrimage $19.99
St. Joseph Hospital $19.99
Ottumwa $19.99
Ottumwa Postcards $19.99
Inklings $19.99
The Narrow Gate $19.99
Days Gone By $19.99
Coming Up Dry $19.99

*Visit our website at www.pbllimited.com to view these and other titles.*

Please add 7 percent sales tax (Iowa residents) and $5.00 per order for mailing in the United States. Send check or money order to PBL Limited, P.O. Box 935, Ottumwa IA 52501-0935.